2

PREVENTING
YOUTH VIOLENCE

Also by Raymond B. Flannery, Jr., Ph.D.

Becoming Stress-Resistant
through the Project SMART Program

Post-Traumatic Stress Disorder:
The Victim's Guide to Healing and Recovery

Violence in the Workplace

The Assaulted Staff Action Program (ASAP):
Coping with the Psychological Aftermath of Violence

Violence in America:
Coping with Drugs, Distressed Families,
Inadequate Schooling, and Acts of Hate

RAYMOND B. FLANNERY, JR., PH.D.

PREVENTING YOUTH VIOLENCE

A Guide for Parents, Teachers, and Counselors

Foreword by Marcia Scott, M.D.

CONTINUUM | NEW YORK

1999
The Continuum Publishing Company
370 Lexington Avenue, New York, NY 10017

Printed in the United States of America

Library of Congress Cataloging-in-Publication Data

Flannery, Raymond B.
    Preventing youth violence : a guide for parents, teachers, and
counselors / Raymond B. Flannery.
    Foreword by Marcia Scott, M.D.
        p. cm.
    Includes bibliographical references (p.   ) and index.
    ISBN 0-8264-1148-7 (alk. paper)
    1. Violence in children—United States—Prevention.
2. Children and violence—United States—Prevention.
3. Problem youth—United States—Psychology.   I. Title.
RJ506.V56F56   1999
618.92'8582—dc21   98-49543
                                                                        CIP

For Young People Everywhere
That They May Always Have Hope

Contents

Foreword

Every time I read one of Raymond Flannery's books I call and tell him that he's written a novel more convincing than real life; that if only he would give it a different title, it would sell like a novel and make him, finally, a rich man. Those of you fortunate enough to have found this book will see what I mean. The stories are absorbing and the characterizations rich. Extensive statistics emerge as illustrations of real-life situations rather than as a journalistic assault. His presentations of theory are like dialogue between concerned characters—"I believe the warning signals (of violence) can be arranged on a continuum of severity from early warning signs that reflect disruptions in reasonable mastery, caring attachments, and the loss of meaningful purpose in life through the serious warning signs of depression, substance abuse, and Posttraumatic Stress Disorder (PTSD), to the urgent warning signs of conduct disorder." And the title of a potential novel is contained in his admonition, "We are not helpless in the face of violence."

But this is not a novel. Dr. Flannery uses the characters and stories to illustrate where and how to look for the warning signs of violence. Without lecturing, he clarifies these signs for those who say, helplessly, that we cannot predict violence. When he tells the step-by-step story of Yummy, the boy who loved candy, the newborn who was persistently scarred and burned, and who met his end execution style at eleven, he does not mean to inflame—"An eleven-year-old killer garners little sympathy." The story is meant to illustrate that while violence does not always beget violence, in certain soil acts of violence are bred by the same motives that breed reasonable behavior. In Yummy's case, his need to belong leads him to a gang; his need to be competent leads him to killing gang enemies; his need to trust eventuates in his being executed by gang members as their competent way of keeping him quiet. The stories breach our denial but are not judgmental. Yummy's membership in a gang calls up class issues. But Michelle, the fifteen-year-old prostitute who left home only after the dog she was protecting from her abusive stepfather finally died of old age, was middle class. And Michelle's parents are presented not only as perpetrators but victims—victims of what I call "commercial slavery" in our postindustrial society.

The later, more serious warning signs—depression, drug use, and psychological pain illustrated by PTSD—are used to integrate psychological, biological, and social theories of violence in ways that are neither belabored nor simplistic. Dr. Flannery's psychological definitions, while instructive for parents and other concerned general readers who too often see only the behavior, will not offend experts. He does not say that depression causes violence but describes depression so that anyone can spot its impact: the impact not of sadness or low mood but of unreasonable self-hate, ebbing energy, loss of contact, and confusion of mind. He does not say that drugs or inner pain cause violence, but links the drug involvement, excitement, and relief of pain with inevitable habituation and loss of control. He *does* say that there is a spectrum of biological and social vulnerability behind the behavior, but he does not back off from his stand that we are not helpless in the face of the precursors to violence—painful frustration, deprivation, and poor coping skills bred by violent example.

Dr. Flannery's most concerned admonitions deal with the warning signs embodied in conduct disorder. Although he wants to know if the conduct is part of a pattern of antisocial behavior, an understandable but deadly response to danger real or perceived, a product of limited ability to solve problems, or a result of common psychiatric disorders, he assures us that we must first stop the behavior. When I worked with explosive children, some too explosive to tolerate protection, able to reconnect only when they could keep their defenses intact through activity and abuse, I found working with them more hopeful than working with those who were without energy. But even then, I knew that for some there was a way back and for some it was only possible to turn a murderer into a white-collar criminal.

The book doesn't dwell extensively on the usual explanation of violence—that a breakdown in our civil society is responsible for increasingly early, dangerous responses to parental and social abuse.

Parental and social violence have always been far more common than we know. But life for children has become more dangerous because of the loss of civility and community. When I was twelve, it *was* safe for me to take the train from New Jersey to New York to go to a museum. Now every parent understands that his or her child is a hostage to fortune. In the 1960s and 1970s, I worked in schools, the barrio, and in children's prisons. I felt safe then but I'm sure I no longer would. I also recall a recent incident in an innocent island community in Maine where the drug dealers considered shooting the kids who were going "to blow their cover" during a drug drop. The dealers decided they couldn't because they were all related by marriages over the past two-hundred years.

Civility and community matter but I think Dr. Flannery does not take the usual tack of bemoaning their loss since, in his eyes, they are more effect than cause. I think his message is that to a large extent, the violence epidemic is a product of our failure to be appalled by it and our failure to do something about it every day. We deserve the civility we make. That's why the most important portions of the book are chapters three to six, which Dr. Flannery recommends to parents. It's not a how-to list. Again using stories, he illustrates how the low-budget moments in life—when parents, teachers, counselors, and cops, even those working two jobs and themselves frustrated—can foster attachment, increase mastery, and give life meaningful purpose for a child. Of course, even he cannot say how we can foster attachment, mastery, and meaning in the parents who themselves suffer frustration and deprivation. But as Dr. Steven E. Hyman, director of the National Institute of Mental Health, has asked when trying to explain the biology of drug abuse: Where does illness end and responsibility begin?

Marcia Scott, M.D.
Child Psychiatrist
Adjunct Faculty,
Beth Israel Hospital, Boston

Introduction

The Problem

The guns fall silent. The victims are taken to the mortuary. Their friends and colleagues are in shock. The killers are removed to jail. As difficult as this is to comprehend, it is even more frightening when we consider that the victims, friends, and killers all have one thing in common: they are children.

Violence in the United States has been increasing steadily since the early 1960s, and has now become a national public health epidemic. Increasingly, much of this violence is committed by our children and our teenagers. Crimes by our young people are no longer predominantly misdemeanors, but now include the major felonies of homicide, rape, robbery, and serious assault. As a nation, we watch in horror at the daily reports of drive-by shootings by teenagers, the murder of students by students, the senseless assaults and robberies by individual youngsters and youth groups, and the continuing aftermath of rapes of children by children.

As citizens, we are understandably concerned by what those in the legal field refer to as the *depraved indifference* of many of our youth. We ask ourselves how this can be happening in a nation so blessed with material goods and choices. These assailants are children in our own neighborhoods. We know them. We know their parents. They seem to be good families. How are we to understand this mayhem?

Having counseled and studied the needs of victims and the minds of their assailants for thirty years, I have been equally distressed by a second question that often accompanies these outbursts: Why were there no warning signs? It has been my experience and that of other counselors that there are warning signs. Frequently, there are several warning signs, and, often, they have been present for many years. I believe that these warning signs can be arranged on a continuum of severity from early warning signs that reflect disruptions in reasonable mastery, caring attachments to others, and the loss of a meaningful purpose in life through the serious warning signs of depression, substance abuse, and untreated Posttraumatic Stress Disorder, to the urgent warning signs of conduct disorder, the juvenile precursor to adult antisocial personality disorder. While no one can predict violence with one hundred percent accuracy, if we understand the warning signs, there are steps that we can then take to prevent further national tragedy. The challenge is to recognize the warning signs, and not to minimize them when we see them. While no one can eliminate every act of aggression, there are helpful things we can do to curtail much of this violence by our young people.

This Book

This book is the first to address the continuum of warning signs and what can be done to prevent violent outbursts by our young. Part 1 describes the extent of violence by young people in the community, in school, and at home, and outlines the various factors that are linked to these aggressive acts. Part 2 presents the continuum of early, serious, and urgent warning signs: what they are and how they come about. Chapter 3, the chapter on the early warning signs, also discusses the normal developmental processes in children that can go awry and that then form the basis of many of the warning signs. Finally, Part 3 describes the process of assessing what the problem is, and the five basic guidelines that are helpful in correcting the underlying problems that have led to the warning signs. The guidelines for intervention have been designed for the greatest flexibility in creating a specific solution for the needs of a specific youngster. The information on the causes of violence in chapter 2 and the process of normal development in chapter 3 may prove of particular importance in developing successful remedies.

The Audience

This book is written for parents, teachers, and counselors, those on the front lines of this war on violence. Counselors and teachers will want to read the entire book for a full overview of the problem and its solutions. Parents with immediate concerns about their children may want to begin with chapters 3 through 6, and return to the more theoretical material later on.

Rearing and educating good children is an enormously complicated task in the best of times. It is even more difficult in today's world with life stresses and rates of change not encountered by previous parents, teachers, and counselors. With this in mind, I have written this book in succinct format. It is also fully referenced with state-of-the-art scientific findings for readers who wish to examine some aspect of youth violence in greater detail. The information in the book coupled with ongoing observation of the troubled child should help with successful interventions. At the end of the book I have included a tear sheet that summarizes the warning signs. This summary can be tacked to the refrigerator door at home or left on one's desk at work, and can serve as a ready reminder.

We are not helpless in the face of violence by our young people. A knowledge of the warning signs and the guidelines for interventions outlined in these pages can help us curb our national epidemic.

Our children must not become an endangered species.

An author's intellectual roots are found in many different sources. I would like to thank my patients and my students for the many things that they have taught me about violence and victimization over the course of several years. I also owe a special debt of gratitude to the following men and women who have provided important academic, clinical, or administrative support: Paul Appelbaum, M.D.; Paul Barreira, M.D.; Joseph Coyle, M.D.; Robert Dorwart, M.D.; George Everly, Jr., Ph.D.; Wallace Haley, Jr.; M.D.; Adrienne Knowles, R.N.; Fotini Lomke; Jeffrey T. Mitchell, Ph.D.; Walter Penk, Ph.D.; Mark Root, R.N.; Mollie Schoenberg; Marylou Sudders, L.I.C.S.W.; and James Woods, S.J., Ed.D. I have been especially fortunate in having the assistance of the following persons in developing the book itself: at Continuum, Evander Lomke, my editor, who correctly perceived the need for this book, as well as Bruce Cassiday, Gene Gollogly, Ulla Schnell, Janna Siegel, and Martin Rowe; my wife Georgina who has served as librarian, researcher, and indexer for various parts of this manuscript; and Judith Bradley who typed the manuscript and served as gentle critic. They have offered wise advice, but any errors remain my sole responsibility.

This book is dedicated to all of our children that they may always have hope during difficult days.

Raymond B. Flannery, Jr., Ph.D., F.A.P.M.
Autumn 1998

Author's Note and Editorial Method

Youth violence with its often co-occurring states of depression, substance abuse, Posttraumatic Stress Disorder, and conduct disorder is a rapidly expanding area of medical and behavioral science inquiry. Medicines and other forms of treatment are constantly being upgraded and the latest research findings should be considered. General guidelines and principles are presented here, but this book is not intended to be a substitute for the advice of the child's physician or professional counselor. Additionally, some child rearing issues may be affected by local law and policies, and some may require legal counsel. Such advice should be heeded. Ultimately, the adult care provider is the person responsible for daily judgments about the child's needs. Raise any questions that you may have with the child's physician, professional counselor, or attorney, and always weigh and follow that advice first.

All of the psychiatric conditions noted in this text may be found and studied in greater detail in the American Psychiatric Association's *Diagnostic and Statistical Manual of Mental Disorders*, Fourth Edition (1994).

• • •

The Select Readings list, which is provided at the end of the volume, contains all of the citations in the book. Citations in the text are listed by the name(s) and year of the publication and may similarly be found in the Readings list.

• • •

All of the examples in this book are based on real events that have happened to real young people. Identifying information in the case histories discussed has been omitted to the extent that this has been possible.

PART ONE

YOUTH VIOLENCE: ITS GENERAL NATURE

Dateline: West Paducah, Kentucky. December 1, 1997.

The Lord is my shepherd, I shall not want.

The day began with sunshine. The forty-six-year-old father of two began yet another day of labored breathing as his terminally diseased lungs continued to fail him. A young girl, age fourteen, was having her final breakfast, although she did not know that at the time; and a second teenaged girl, age fifteen, was dashing off to school, similarly unaware that a piece of metal smaller than her thumb would this day end her dashing about forever.

In another home across town, a young boy, age fourteen, had finally focused his anger. No more secrets, no more teasing, he thought, five guns will more than earn me their respect.

Even though I walk through the valley of the shadow of death, I shall fear no evil.

Thirty-five high school students were saying their final amens in their early morning, voluntary prayer group, when the young boy's hail of automatic gunfire disbanded the group into individual pools of blood. Three, including the first young girl, died with love in their hearts and prayers on their lips. Five others remained wounded, including the second teenage girl, who would now be paralyzed for life.

Surely goodness and mercy shall follow me all the days of my life.

Has the world gone crazy?

He was a quiet kid. They seemed like such a nice family.

How could this happen?

Why, God? Why?

And I will dwell in the house of the Lord forever.

Honoring their daughter's last request, the parents of the first young girl opened what was left of their unspeakably broken hearts, and donated their daughter's vital organs that others might live.

Thus, the father of two with the failing lungs received life in the midst of death.

Notwithstanding, it remained dark.

Here is one example of an unspeakable act of youth violence. Sadly, it is not alone. Our nation's youth continues to commit acts of homicide, rape, robbery, and assault along with the variety of lesser crimes. In beginning our study of the nature of youth violence, let us consider the following questions:

1. Can this really be happening in a land of so many material goods and plurality of choices?
2. Does this youth violence cut across gender and age?
3. Why does there seem to be so much violence by our young people now?
4. What makes children act like this? Are they all mentally ill?
5. What does this violence do to the children who are victims and witnesses of this carnage?

1

CHILDREN: OUR ENDANGERED SPECIES

The horror. The horror.
—Joseph Conrad

Man has discovered death.
—W. B. Yeats

No! . . . No! . . . Not again! . . .

Some had heard it on the news. Some had received phone calls. Others learned of it as word spread throughout the neighborhood.

From home and office, a phalanx of parents instinctively raced to the middle school that had seemed so idyllic just a few short hours ago. Minds numb with terror. Hearts frozen in fear. They approached the last one hundred yards to the school grounds, and each knew that he or she would be greeted with the agony of death or the mixed joy and terror of knowing that his or her child had survived—this time.

Please, God, not my little one. . . .

The scene was painfully familiar. Flashing lights. Police. Emergency services personnel. Spattered blood. Lifeless young bodies. Spent bullets. Teachers who were immobilized. Students who walked aimlessly in tears. Students who were angered. Students who had helplessly withdrawn into their own personal darkness.

The police and emergency services personnel continued with their grim task. Staunching blood, where first aid was possible. Transporting small lifeless bodies, where it was not. Small lifeless bodies that served as painful reminders of their own children.

Bethel, AL. Pearl, MS. West Paducah, KY. Jonesboro, AK. Edinboro, PA. Springfield, OR. Richmond, VA.

The children of the United States had declared war on the country's young, and the nation's schools had become part of the killing fields of the new millennium.

Violence in the United States has become a national public health epidemic. Our communities, our offices and factories, our schools, and even our own homes are no longer necessarily safe. Included in the national statistics on crime has been a sharp increase in violence by youth. As the chapter vignette suggests, our young people have moved beyond misdemeanors to the four major crimes of homicide, rape, robbery, and serious assault. Consider the following national survey drawn at random:

- Providence, RI.—A four-year-old is in the hospital with a bullet lodged near its spinal cord, the victim of a drive-by shooting.
- Brooklyn, NY.—A ten-year-old girl is arrested for stealing a wallet from a purse. It is her nineteenth arrest.
- Minneapolis, MN.—A nine-year-old girl murders the infant for whom she was baby-sitting.
- Lone Oaks, KY.—A high school senior is arrested for threatening to kill the baseball coach who did not put him on the team.
- Fayetteville, TN.—A high school student kills another student in an argument over a girl three days before graduation.
- Dallas, TX.—Three young boys rob a house for a purse and some whiskey, and kill the fifty-two-year-old homemaker by slitting her throat.
- Pocatello, ID.—A fourteen-year-old boy at a school for troubled youth pulls a gun on the principal, and proceeds to trash an entire school building.
- San Francisco, CA.—Two male and six female high school students terrorize and intimidate a teenage girl. Their violence includes rape and robbery.

Violence is usually defined as the use of physical force to injure or abuse another person or verbal acts that seek to cause physical or emotional harm to a person or object. By these definitions, for too many of our children, it is an unacceptably violent world. Not only are they subject to unprecedented levels of adult predatory behaviors that include homicide, physical and sexual assault, verbal threats, and neglect, but children must now be on the alert for these same aggressive behaviors among their peers. In Indianapolis, an elementary school becomes the first to put in metal detectors. In Long Beach, a junior high school builds a solid wall around the school grounds. In cities across the country, large and small, children are afraid to walk to school, the store, or the playground. The toll in death, injury, and human suffering is considerable.

This first chapter examines the extent of violence committed by our young people, and focuses primarily on the major crimes of homicide, rape, robbery, and serious assault. While there have been recent and encouraging reductions in these crimes due in part to the aging of the baby-boomer generation, community policing, longer prison sentences, programs to remove guns and drugs from the street, and enhanced youth programs, the frequency of these serious crimes still remain at unacceptably high levels. Moreover, the statistics that are reported may be underestimated because not all victims of violence report what has happened to them. Some do not realize that they are victims of crime (e.g., date-rape victims). Others fear retaliation or are too ashamed to come forward. Still others believe that nothing will come from their reporting of violent acts. Therefore, it is reasonable to assume that the violent behavior to be reported in this chapter, as alarming as it is, is probably still under-represented.

Joseph Conrad perhaps said it best. To study violence is to journey deeper and deeper into the heart of darkness. Let us begin with a review of the extent of the problem in order to understand fully what needs to be addressed.

The Nature of Youth Violence in America

Youth Violence: In the Community

Since crime statistics fluctuate from year to year, we need some method to analyze trends in crime and violence over time. Toward that end, I have constructed tables 1-4 from national crime data compiled by statistician Andrew Dobrin and his colleagues (Dobrin, Wiersema, Loftin, and McDowall, 1996). Unlike our own day, the

TABLE 1

Comparative Crime Statistics: 1960, 1965, and 1992:

Type of Crime	1960	Victims* 1965	1992
Homicide	5.2	6.2	10.5
Rape	8.7	11.6	42.8
Robbery	49.6	61.4	263.6
Assault	72.6	106.6	441.8

*Rates per 100,000

early 1960s were low-crime years, and serve as a helpful reference point in gauging recent levels of crime and violence. With the exception of the homicide statistics in table 1, which are from the National Center for Health Statistics, all data are from the Uniform Crime Report (UCR) of the FBI.

Table 1 presents a comparison of the various crime rates for the years 1960, 1965, and 1992. The year 1965 has been included to reflect the beginning of the sharp increases in violent crime with which we are now confronted. Tables 2-4 begin with the year 1965, and already reflect increases in crime from the low-violence period of the late 1950s and early 1960s.

There has been a staggering increase in crime during the past thirty-five years in all categories of violence. The findings are grim. The homicide rate has doubled, rapes and robberies have increased fivefold, and the assault rate has increased sixfold. Although some of these increases may in part reflect more accurate reporting, these data also reflect true increases in the levels of these offenses, and are still subject to the problem of underreporting that we have noted.

As sobering as these statistics are, they mask two further serious factors: sharp increases in violence by youth, and a corresponding increase in violent behavior by young girls.

TABLE 2

Youth and Adult Crime Statistics: 1965 and 1992:

	Victims*	
Type of Crime	1965	1992
Homicide		
Over 18	8.3	10.4
Under 18	1.4	5.0
Rape		
Over 18	10.5	16.9
Under 18	4.9	9.3
Robbery		
Over 18	39.7	68.7
Under 18	30.3	70.5
Assault		
Over 18	88.5	227.1
Under 18	28.5	112.8

*Rates per 100,000

While the high-crime years for any generation are ages fifteen to twenty-four, society tends to think of youth as persons under eighteen years of age. Table 2 outlines the four major offenses for the years 1965 and 1992. The data reflect not only the increases in adult criminal behavior, but also dramatic increases in youth violence during the same period. The data for youth additionally reflect greater percentage increases in violence for each category as compared to the data for adults. The youth homicide and assault rates increased almost fourfold, while the rates for rape and robbery doubled. The perception of increased youth violence is accurately grounded in our national data.

Table 3 continues our examination of violence by young people by presenting the violence data for children under age eighteen by gender for the years 1965 and 1992. Again, the data reflect dramatic increases in violence for each category of offense for both boys and girls. For boys, homicides and assaults increase fourfold, rape in-

TABLE 3

Youth Crime Statistics (Under 18) by Gender: 1965 and 1992:

Type of Crime	Victims*			
	Male Assailants		Female Assailants	
	1965	1992	1965	1992
Homicide	2.6	9.3	0.2	0.6
Rape	9.7	17.8	0.0	0.4
Robbery	56.9	125.9	2.8	12.3
Assault	48.9	183.9	7.3	38.3

*Rates per 100,000

creases twofold, and robberies increase threefold. While the total number of girls involved in violent behavior is still well below the number of boys, there are still unacceptably high levels of violence by girls, and the percentage increase in recent years by girls has surpassed the recent increase by boys.

Finally, table 4 outlines the level of violence for the truly young—girls and boys under age fourteen. Again the findings are cause for serious concern. Even the youngest of our children are involved in our national public health epidemic of violence. Many appear to have turned against society, an event that bodes ill for them, ill for the youth who are not violent, and ill for our nation as a whole.

Youth Violence: At School

Most adults leave their communities in the morning and go to work. For most children, the analogous activity is to go to school. However, schools are no longer necessarily safe havens, and many children are understandably frightened in their classrooms.

From data based on a sample of 1,200 public schools, a 1998 Department of Education report estimated that in one academic year

TABLE 4

Youth Crime Statistics (Under 14) by Gender: 1965 and 1992:

Type of Crime	Male Assailants		Female Assailants	
	Victims*			
	1965	1992	1965	1992
Homicide				
12–14	3.7	8.7	0.2	0.9
0–11	0.1	0.1	**	**
Rape				
12–14	15.4	44.0	**	**
0–11	0.7	2.8	**	**
Robbery				
12–14	129.5	258.1	9.4	37.5
0–11	10.3	10.6	0.7	1.1
Assault				
12–14	93.2	370.5	22.7	105.1
0–11	7.4	24.4	1.5	4.5

*Rates per 100,000
**Rates are less than 0.05

there were 11,000 fights in which weapons were used, 4,000 rapes and other sexual assaults, and 7,000 robberies. In 1997, over 6,000 guns were confiscated from students, a figure that included 500 weapons that were brought to school by elementary school students.

Equally distressing is the increase in gang activity, since much of it involves drug dealing with and/or robberies of school students. An Education and Justice Department survey of the years from 1989 to 1995 found that the number of students reporting the presence of gangs rose from 24.8 percent to 40.7 percent in central cities, from 14.0 percent to 26.3 percent in suburban areas, and from 7.8 percent to 19.9 percent in nonmetropolitan and rural areas. This was accompanied by 7.5 percent increase in the number of student victims who reported gangs in their schools in 1995 as compared to 2.7 percent of students in schools with no gangs.

In an attempt to cope with these increasingly unsafe school environments, many students now take special routes to school, avoid certain places in the school or on its grounds, stay together in groups at school, or avoid possible violence in school altogether by staying home. Others carry weapons for self-defense.

Youth Violence: At Home

Data on home violence is more difficult to ascertain because much of it is inflicted by parents on children who are afraid to report it. However, some data is available on homicides, abductions, and physical and sexual assaults.

Social scientists Jennifer Kunz and Stephen Bahr (1996) completed a study on parental homicide from UCR data for the years 1976 to 1985. During these years there were 3,459 children under age eighteen who were killed by a parent. In the first week of the child's life, the mother almost always committed the murder; by the time the child was age sixteen, the father committed the murder in 80 percent of the cases. Personal weapons, asphyxiation, and drowning were the likely weapons among the very youngest victims, with guns and knives becoming the predominant weapons as the age of the child increased.

The children who survive often do not fare much better. The United States Department of Justice reports an estimated 354,000 family abductions of children each year, with 160,000 of those parents planning to keep the stolen child for an indefinite period of time. Estimates of child sexual abuse by parents or significant other adults in the home range from 20 percent for all girls to 10-15 percent for all boys.

In perhaps the most thorough findings to date, sociologists Murray Straus and Richard Gelles (1992) conducted a national family survey of 6,002 families in 1985. Their findings included extensive evidence of familial violence: 161 per 1,000 couples experienced one or more physical assaults. In 34 per 1,000 cases, these assaults were so severe that they constituted wife battering. Women were as equally likely to initiate this violence as men, and there were 24 per 1,000 episodes of severe child abuse committed by these parents.

The children who were witnesses to, or direct victims of, this parental violence themselves became violent. Almost half of the younger children had hit one sibling, and 20 percent had attacked a parent. The teenagers in these families (ages fifteen to seventeen) were also violent with two-thirds hitting a sibling and 10 percent assaulting a parent (Straus and Gelles, 1992).

Youth Violence: Unanswered Questions

The data on violence by young people leave at least two important questions as yet unanswered.

The first question is that of the presence of a core group of youth who may be responsible for a disproportionate amount of these overall levels of crime. This question stems from research begun by criminologist Marvin Wolfgang (Wolfgang, Figlio, and Sellin, 1972). In 1945, Dr. Wolfgang and his colleagues recorded the births of all males in the city of Philadelphia. They followed this group of 9,945 males until they reached their eighteenth birthdays, and recorded any encounters that these children had with the police. About two-thirds of the subjects had no involvement with the police. Of the remaining 35 percent, half had committed one delinquent or criminal act and had no further involvement with the police. Two-thirds of the other half had two to four more encounters before their eighteenth birthday. However, 627 were arrested five or more times. This small group was disproportionately committing a large percentage of all serious crime. (No females were included in this study.)

It is not known from the national data reported here whether a small percentage of youth is still responsible for the larger percentage of these crimes in our own age, and we have no knowledge of whether there is a similar phenomenon for female delinquent youth. If there is still a core delinquent group, then parents, teachers, and counselors might logically focus their prevention efforts on this small group. In the event that youth violence has become more generally widespread, then many youths will need to be assessed for possible help. In the present absence of data for such a core group, the wiser strategy is to assess the needs of *all* youth.

A second unanswered question is the presence of so many violent female youths. Girls who seldom fought with fists now use knives, razors, box cutters, guns, and the like in their pursuit of power, status, dominance, recognition, and a wide variety of material resources. Until recently, however, females, including young girls, have often relied on strategies that have included instigation, duplicity, lying, neglect, and setting others up. What is more recent is the common use of physical force to obtain one's ends in arguments over boys, clothes, and getting ahead. Are girls learning by modeling the violent behaviors of boys? Do girls have greater access to a variety of weapons, and, thus, tend to use them? Why does violence in girls often begin in adolescence, whereas it may manifest itself in boys at earlier ages?

We do not know, and research is urgently needed on these matters.

The data on youth violence across community, school and home settings are clear, consistent, and chilling. *Our children do not feel safe because they are not safe.*

The Impact of Violence on Youth

The pain and suffering inflicted on victims is both extensive and depressing. The victims include victims of direct acts of violence, witnesses of violence inflicted on others, and family members and other loved ones who must help the victim and themselves cope with the aftermath of hatred.

The first impact of violence may be physical injury or dismemberment. Violent acts may result in death, permanent disability, medical injury, and medical and legal expense. If young people are the victims, the resulting aftermath may lead to lost time from school, from extracurricular activities, and from part-time or full-time work. For parents, lost productivity may result in time away from work to attend to the medical and legal needs of their child victims. For teachers and counselors, it may mean absence from the classroom from one's own personal fears for safety or for time spent in addressing the needs of student victims.

Injuries eventually heal. Lawsuits are completed. Victims and their families return to work. In many cases, young victims get on with their lives. But not always.

There is a second aspect of the impact of violence. It is the mental anguish that may accompany violent acts that result in psychological trauma. Initially, this suffering may be associated with feeling stunned, terrified, and very angry. It is often accompanied by hypervigilance, disturbed sleep, and intrusive memories of the event, symptoms of a medical condition known as Acute Stress Disorder. If it is left untreated, which is often the case, there is a high probability that it may evolve into Posttraumatic Stress Disorder (PTSD)(Flannery, 1994a). Untreated PTSD lasts until death. Psychological trauma is a very serious matter and a common outcome after youth violence, and it is discussed at greater length in chapter 4.

The third impact of violence is the transmission of violence inflicted by one generation on another generation. This *intergenerational transfer of violence* occurs when parents abuse their children, and those same children then go on to abuse others as they become adults. Psychologist Cathy Spatz Widom (1989) has studied this problem rigorously. She began by collecting information on cases of child abuse (physical and sexual abuse, neglect) filed in a county juvenile court from the years 1967 to 1971. For each case of an abused child, she then found a nonabused child from the county birth records that matched the abused child on sex, age, race, and level of family income. Twenty years later she then examined a variety of local, state, and federal court records to see if the abused children and their matched control cohorts had been involved in any subsequent crimes. In comparison with the nonabused children, about a quarter of the abused children had more arrests for juvenile crimes, more arrests for adult crimes, and still more arrests for violent offenses. The children who had been victims of physical abuse had higher levels of arrest for violent crime than did victims of neglect. These children had learned to be violent at home, and used violence as adults to solve problems.

These findings indicate that being a victim of violence may in itself be a precursor to a variety of violent behaviors by the victim at a subsequent time in the victim's life.

The End of Childhood?

Former university English professor and social essayist Wendell Berry (1995) says that, as a society, we speak a good deal about our commitment to children, but in many cases the facts speak otherwise. Since many children are sensitive to these mixed messages, the paradox may explain some of the violence committed by our young people.

While the culture speaks of the importance of its children, Dr. Berry and others (e.g., Hewlett, 1991) have noted that these children are murdered, mutilated, abandoned, physically and sexually abused, drugged, neglected, and sometimes poorly clothed, fed, and housed. They are victims of inadequate prenatal and day care, forced labor, drive-by shootings, and inadequate health insurance. These are not indicators of young lives free from unnecessary stress.

As our young people look toward the future, they correctly perceive that they will inherit serious parental debt, a polluted environment, a failing infrastructure, no national parental-leave policy, and an insufficient Social Security retirement system. Dr. Berry is not asking the adult world to solve all of the nation's problems, but he is suggesting that we be firm in our commitment to our young people.

This completes our frightening overview of youth violence. Our young people are regularly involved in the most heinous of crimes, and these young assailants are from all age groups, both genders, all social classes, all races, all ethnic groups, and all religious denominations.

The evil of violence has no favorites in terms of either victims or assailants. Violent children are at higher risk for alcohol and substance abuse, for adult crime, and for personal lives marked by divorce, dysfunctional families, and inadequate employment. Moreover, the pain and suffering that they inflict on their victims is enormous, and can last a lifetime in the lives of innocent children who were the wrong persons in the wrong place at the wrong time. There are no winners in the face of violence.

The presence of so many angry children tells us that something is dreadfully amiss, and the next chapter begins to address why young people with the greatest amount of material goods and life choices in the history of the human family place themselves and others in harm's way. We turn now to the theories of youth violence to understand its causes, and to reflect on what the theories may have to teach us about prevention.

2

ARMED AND DANGEROUS:
THEORIES OF YOUTH VIOLENCE

Cruelty has a human heart.
—William Blake

If you wish peace, understand war.
—Lidell Hart

Little Henry sat rigidly in silence like the good little soldier that he was. It was hard for an eight-year-old to sit still, but he forced himself to do so because the consequences of the slightest noise were so frightening.

His eyes darted furtively to the corner of the room. The angry eyes, the labored breathing, the stern face confirmed his worst fears.

What made it all the more difficult just now was his need to clear his throat. How to do this without making a sound? He took a deep breath very slowly. It did not help. He tried to swallow hard, but that did not work either.

When the refrigerator motor went on, little Henry froze in horror. The eyes and the voice in the other corner of the room became enraged at the sound, and this wrathful force headed toward the kitchen.

Henry tried to head off his drunken father, but was thrown against the stairwell banister with a force that cut his facial cheek. In the kitchen, Henry's drunken father began to beat his mother once again. It terrified him when his mother's face became covered with blood. Once again, he tried to separate them. Once again, he was thrown aside, and smashed head first into the oven door. His jaw and teeth began to really hurt.

Surely Reverend Brown must be wrong. How could God expect us to love everyone?

His jaw and teeth remained etched in pain, and his small brown eyes were filled with deep sadness.

Why do children and adults do these things to one another? Are they not in their right minds? Could people really be this mean? Even young children?

No one can predict violent behavior with full accuracy, because each violent act is a complex piece of behavior that results from several factors that coalesce at one moment in time. There are many possible pathways to the eruption of aggression. However, this does not mean that the root causes of these events cannot be understood in many cases. In the instance of little Henry's family, parental alcoholism and a past history of parental violence toward others are both factors known to be related to high-risk situations for violence.

This chapter focuses on those factors known to be associated with subsequent acts of violence in youth. They fall into four categories: (1) cultural factors that are associated with values and major shifts in society, (2) biological factors that identify possible biological and medical roots of aggression, (3) sociological factors that focus on social ills that manifest themselves in crime and violence, and (4) psychological factors that highlight the skills and motivational state of the assailant. Since these matters are covered in great detail for the interested reader elsewhere (Flannery, 1997), this overview presents the main findings and the most likely types of violence that are apt to occur in each category.

There has been a lengthy debate in medicine, behavioral science, and philosophy over which of these four groupings of factors is the most important in understanding human behavior, including the human violence by young people that we have just reviewed. One group, the Nature group, believes that the biological factors are of the greatest consequence. They consider that a person's genetic and biological makeup at birth in large part shape the destiny of that individual's life. A second group, the Nurture group, emphasizes the importance of the cultural, sociological, and psychological factors in determining how a person will behave. This long-standing controversy is known as the Nature-Nurture argument, and applies to our understanding of the behavior of youth as well as that of adults. A review of the Nature-Nurture research findings on violence (Flannery, 1997) suggests that, with the relatively rare exception of certain medical conditions, most violent acts have components of both Nature and Nurture, and this sense of complexity should guide our efforts in trying to understand angry youth.

Since there appears to be no one single way to understand violence, our search for prevention strategies will also need to be multifaceted. The various factors associated with youth violence are attempts to help us understand the breeding grounds for antisocial behavior. It is from these breeding grounds that the warning signs of violence among the young emerge. The greater our understanding of the implications of these factors is, the better will be our awareness of how the warning signs can be successfully addressed before violence erupts.

Adults know from daily personal experience that ours is an age of rapid social change and intense personal life stress. The same is true for our children, so our review of the theories of violence begins by examining how cultural factors may be contributing to the grim statistics of violence by our young people.

Cultural Factors

The Postindustrial State

The United States and the other nations of the world are in the midst of an enormous and basic cultural shift as the peoples of the world are becoming interwoven in a global economy and a worldwide communication network. The impact on individual lives has been deeply felt. In our own country, this shift has occurred in the transition from an industrial-based society to an information-based society.

The period of the 1850s in our history is known as the Industrial Revolution, and marks the point in our national development when energy was harnessed to machines. Water power to run the spinning looms was shortly followed by steam, coal, oil, electricity, and thermal and nuclear energies that have been harnessed to a variety of machinery over the years, and our economy and quality of life improved greatly (Sagan, 1987).

The 1970s marked the shift from the industrial state to the new postindustrial state with its emphasis on knowledge and continuous information processing in such areas as biotechnology, microelectronics, and health care. The new emphasis on research and development to remain competitive in the new global economy has led to the development of three work-related groupings in society: the knowledge workers who conduct the needed cutting-edge research; the support services employees who support their efforts in fields such as banking, financing, transportation, communications, and energy; and the permanent underclass, comprised of those without the education and skills needed to function in either of the first two groups. The members of the permanent underclass are underemployed, unemployed, and poor. (The interested reader is referred to Drucker [1994] and Thurow [1996] for more detailed analyses.)

This shift in the economy has also been accompanied by a major shift in values. While the former industrial state was characterized by values that included hard work, honesty, self-denial, self-control, sexual exclusivity, and concern for the welfare of one's family and one's neighbors, the new poststindustrial state is marked by three different major values. The first is the primacy of the self, a sense of personal entitlement to one's own needs, often with no corresponding sense of responsibility to others or to society as a whole. The second value is expressed in the consumption of material goods and services. Success becomes defined as the accumulation of the greatest number of goods, even after the time constraints needed to enjoy these products has long been surpassed. The final goal or value is that of instant gratification of the body and its senses. Self-denial and delay of gratification have been replaced with an unfettered emphasis on instant sex, drugs, alcohol, gambling, coarse music (e.g.; heavy metal, rap), and a generally highly charged life style.

At least two important questions follow from this short description of this major cultural shift: What happens to those who live through this era? What, if any, are the links of these changes to the rising levels of youth violence that were catalogued in the previous chapter? A partial answer to these questions may be found in the writings of the sociologist, Émile Durkheim (trans. 1951).

Anomie

As a student of human behavior in groups, Durkheim was impressed by the ability of any society's major social institutions to regulate moral behavior in a capitalistic economy. The infinity of desire was held in check by the societal institutions of the family, schools, business, government, and religion. But what happens if the social fabric disintegrates in the face of major societal shifts, such as the one we have outlined here?

In Durkheim's view, as a major shift proceeds, the sense of integrated community is lost. People feel adrift and are no longer closely linked to others in basic social rituals. Durkheim labeled this tendency for social norms to lose their regulatory force *anomie.*

Durkheim's research on the impact of anomie led to the documentation of increases in suicides, substance abuse, general psychological distress, and violent crime, all markers of our own age and especially of our young people who are living through this major shift in social paradigms.

Youth Violence

The cultural theory of anomie may help us to understand some of the youth violence that is currently occurring. Much of today's violence by young people is happening when our children are under the influence of alcohol and other drugs. While this may be a part of the cultural value of instant gratification, it may also be a way of self-medicating the intense loneliness and anger that arises when the social fabrics of home and school are not stable. Much of their random violence may also stem from the disruptions in the guidelines of the regulatory social forces. With no clear rules, some youth may feel overwhelmed and strike out aimlessly in anger at this faceless anomie. Youth suicides and violence toward the self may also be understood in this light. Life seems confusing, no one seems in charge, and a sense of helplessness and hopelessness may lead some to take their own lives.

Violence in the permanent underclass in response to anomie may take the forms of violence for the sake of survival (e.g., armed robbery) or as a less adaptive way of earning a living (e.g., fencing stolen property). These strategies may be necessary for survival, but they involve the young in lifestyles marked by violence.

It is not surprising that major cultural shifts such as the one that society is now experiencing should leave many youths in all social classes feeling confused, abandoned, overwhelmed, and alone. Nor is it unexpected when violence follows in some of them just as it has done historically in earlier periods of major change. Anomie is an important factor in understanding some of our present levels of youth violence, and we shall return to it toward the end of the chapter.

Biological Factors

Genetic/Instincts

Are humans born to be violent and aggressive? This question arose in our country after the horrors of World War II, when reasonable men and women tried to understand how such destruction could have occurred.

Many thoughtful writers of the day believed that humans were born with an instinct to act aggressively toward others in situations other than self-defense. However, over fifty years of research (Flannery, 1997) has failed to document any instinct or genetic propensity other than in situations of self-defense. In fact, some of the latest and most advanced genetic research reveals that any genetic predisposition to violence is complex and may involve many different genes (Bouchard, 1994).

There is no present credible evidence to conclude that today's violent youth are born this way.

Having stated this, it should also be noted that research does indicate that there are some characteristics of temperament that do appear to be inherited and that may predispose some youngsters to crime and violence. Some of the more common and potentially troublesome traits include low intelligence, emotionality, hyperactivity, impulsivity, and sensation seeking. The traits themselves do not cause violence, but the *characteristics* of these traits may place these youngsters in situations where violence may occur.

Medical Conditions

Although there is no evidence of genetic involvement in youth violence, other types of biological factors may be involved in some acts of aggression. These include an array of medical and psychiatric disorders, which are not meant to be exhaustive, but are presented here to acquaint us with the range of issues involved.

The cortex, the limbic system, and the nervous system itself have each been shown to be involved in some cases of youth violence. The cortex is our thinking brain. It receives information through our senses, scans memory for past similar life experiences, plans strategies to resolve whatever problem may be before us, and then implements the plan. The cortex is involved in social learning, moral judgment, and anticipating the consequences of our behavior, the very deficits found in some violent youth. Birth defects, head injuries, viruses, exposure to noxious chemical agents, exposure to metals like lead and mercury, and vitamin deficiencies (B_{12}, folate, thiamine) have all been known to disrupt the brain's functioning and lead to violence in some instances.

The limbic system is embedded under the cortex in the center of the brain, and is one of the major centers in the brain that adds feelings to human experiences. If I am a young boy who is jealous of a classmate, or a young girl who is very angry about failing an exam, I am experiencing these feelings in my limbic system. Two parts of the limbic system, the hypothalamus and the amygdala, have been shown to be activated in people who are angry and full of rage, and thus persistent negative feelings in some youngsters that result in violence may involve the limbic system as one contributing factor. The most recent research on the limbic system and youth reveals one possible additional role of the limbic system in youth violence. Recent medical studies of impulsive behaviors (quick actions without thought) have demonstrated that adults are much more likely to activate and utilize the cortex to solve problems, whereas teenagers are more likely to activate the limbic system with its sometimes impulsive consequences. This may explain in part why fights sometimes suddenly erupt among teenagers (Yurgelun-Todd, 1998). However, these are preliminary findings, and much research remains to be conducted.

The third part of the brain that may be involved in some youth violence are the neurotransmitters that connect the fibers of the nervous system. Our nervous system is not made of long unbroken cords of nerve fiber, rather it is a network of many smaller fibers that are connected by microscopic balloonlike vesicles known as synaptic gaps. These gaps contain chemicals that act like drum heads, and that resonate and transfer the information from one nerve fiber across the synaptic gap to the next nerve fiber, until the information reaches the cortex for resolution. If the chemicals are all present in the correct amounts, the information flow works smoothly. When these chemicals are not in their proper balance, the person does not function effectively, and may become irritable and hyperreactive. This hyperreactivity may result in angry outbursts and violent behavior.

Two important neurotransmitters in the synaptic gaps are epinephrine and norepinephrine. When the body confronts stressful life events, the adrenal glands emit adrenaline that is converted to epinephrine in the body and mobilizes the body's breathing, heart rate, muscle tone, and the like so that it is prepared to fight or flee. At the same time, adrenaline is converted to norepinephrine in the brain, and rivets the person's attention to the crisis at hand so that solving the potentially life-threatening problem is greatly enhanced. Disorders of these neurotransmitters in youth may lead to violence in some.

Finally, a word about the role of the hormone testosterone in men and boys. This hormone is produced in the testes and is found in high concentrations in males between the ages of fifteen and twenty-four, the high crime years in each generation. Testosterone provides increased energy, assertiveness, and sexual arousal, but many consider these benefits to be outweighed by testosterone's perceived association with aggression. As with the research findings on genetics, the most recent studies of the role of testosterone in violence (Archer, 1994) find no clear association between the two. Testosterone by itself does not appear to lead to violence.

Psychiatric Conditions

This next section, briefly examines some of the psychiatric disorders that have been associated with violence in youth. Again, we shall look at some possible types of violent acts that might occur in each condition.

1. *Mental Retardation.* Mental retardation is seriously limited intellectual functioning. The individual has markedly severe deficits in comprehension, understanding, and problem solving. When these youngsters are frustrated by their limited skills, they may become hyperaroused and angry, and assault family members and other care givers.

2. *Attention Deficient/Hyperactivity Disorder (ADHD).* ADHD is a birth disorder characterized by excessive energy and activity, and poor cognitive and behavioral skills. These youngsters may be disorganized, tactless, inattentive, bossy, obstinate, and impulsive. Many of these behaviors are similar in nature to aggressive traits, and some of these youngsters go on to develop substance abuse, conduct disorder, and aggressive behavior toward parents and peers.

3. *Reactive Detachment Disorder.* This disorder of infancy and childhood is marked by severe disturbances in social attachments to others. In failing to relate to a parent or other care giver, the child may fail to initiate activities, fail to respond to adults and remain hypervigilant, or the child may become socially indiscriminate. While this condition is rare, it is caused by persistent disregard of the child's basic emotional needs and is the result of parental neglect.

4. *Serious Mental Illness.* Serious mental illnesses are medical diseases that run in families. They include schizophrenia (disturbances in thought), mania (disturbances in elevated mood states), and recurring major depressive episodes (disturbances in depressed mood states). These illnesses often begin in adolescence, and violence may be associated with these illnesses in differing ways.

Persons with schizophrenia, especially if they are paranoid and have been drinking, become frightened, and assaultive toward family members or health care providers. The person with mania will assault any person who seeks to constrict his or her state of happy excitement. The depressed person may strike out at others in anger, or strike at the self in the form of suicide or other acts of self-mutilation.

5. *Posttraumatic Stress Disorder (PTSD)*. Ironically, people of all ages who have been victims of violence may themselves become perpetrators of violence at some later point, as we have seen. Dr. Widom's data on the intergenerational transfer of violence among youth who were victims in their own homes is one example. Being a victim of sexual assaults in juvenile detention settings or severe physical abuse in school are other examples. Subsequent violent acts from these victims may occur at any time to anyone.

6. *Alcohol/Drug Abuse*. Alcohol and drugs are substances that alter brain chemistry, disinhibit the cortical control centers of the brain that keep violence in check, and interfere with normal reasoning and problem solving. Much of the crime and violence that children commit, experience directly, or witness happening to others is related to substance abuse. Aggression here may result from the direct action of these agents on the brain, from the side effects that arise from these drugs, from the withdrawal effects as these drugs are secreted from the body, or as the result of direct confrontations with the substance abuser whose reasoning is now compromised. In these drug-altered states, husbands kill wives, mothers kill children, teenagers murder each other, and younger children overdose and kill themselves by accident. Any of us can be a victim of violence at the hands of intoxicated youth.

7. *Depression/Suicide*. Serious clinical depression is marked by loss of physical energy and the loss of interest in one's daily activities and goals. Feelings of anger, sadness, guilt, and hopelessness are also often present. Depressed children particularly show sharp increases in irritability and in anhedonia, the absence of pleasure in life's activities. As was noted earlier, some depression is accompanied by serotonin depletion, and may result in violent acts toward others such as shootings, strangulations, drownings, and severe physical

assaults with mutilation as well as violence against the self in the form of repeated acts of self-mutilation, potential self-destruction in high-risk situations, or in completed suicides. Anyone may be a victim of these violent acts. Unrecognized depression in children is a very serious problem.

These psychiatric conditions, and the two personality disorders below, oppositional defiant disorder and conduct disorder, have been summarized in table 1 by type of disorder and usual age of onset.

Personality Disorders

1. *Oppositional Defiant Disorder*. Oppositional defiant disorder is characterized by a recurring pattern of active defiance, disobedience, and open hostility toward adult authority figures. These children are angry and resentful, do not follow the rules, deliberately provoke others, and often blame others for their own mistakes. Frustration tolerance is low and substance abuse may be present. These children display these defiant behaviors at home, at school, and in the neighborhood. This disorder is prevalent in children from homes where there has been a succession of different care givers or where there has been harsh, inconsistent, and neglectful child-rearing practices.

2. *Conduct Disorder*. Conduct disorders are recurring patterns of defiant, antisocial behaviors that are more extreme than those of oppositional defiant disordered children. They include aggressive behavior that causes harm to persons or animals, aggressive behavior that damages property, deceitfulness or theft, and serious violations of the basic rules of society. These children have poor social and academic skills. Some have ADHD and many have been victims of violence themselves at the hands of others. Conduct disordered children constitute our most violent young people.

Although it is true that biological factors may be present in some acts of violence by young people, it is rare for an act of violence to be caused solely by some medical or psychiatric condition. Since these instances are relatively infrequent, they could in no way ac-

TABLE 1

Psychiatric Conditions in Youth Violence:

Psychiatric Disorder	*Age of Onset*
Mental Retardation	Birth
Attention Deficit/ Hyperactivity Disorder	Birth
Reactive Attachment Disorder	Infancy or Early Childhood
Serious Mental Illness	Late Teens Onward
Posttraumatic Stress Disorder	Any Age
Alcohol/Drug Abuse	Any Age
Depression/Suicide	Any Age
Personality Disorder	*Age of Onset*
Oppositional Defiant Disorder	Before Age Fifteen
Conduct disorder	Before Age Fifteen

count for our current epidemic of violence. Our children are not born to be violent nor are they out of their minds when they commit such heinous acts. Even those few with true medical conditions can be adequately treated so that a second act of violence related to the medical disorder need not occur.

Sociological Factors

The sociological factors that are traditionally associated with youth violence are poverty, inadequate schooling, domestic violence, discrimination, substance abuse/easily available weapons, gangs, and the media (e.g., television, movies, music). Given that much of our youth crime is now committed by more affluent youngsters, I would also like to raise briefly for consideration the possible role of the economy in violence by affluent children.

Since these factors are reported frequently in print and in the media (Derber, 1996; Flannery, 1997), most of us are familiar with them. The focus in this section, therefore, will be to provide a brief review of each factor and to concenrate on the types of violence that follow from each of these issues.

The Economy

Poverty. Poverty is defined as not having adequate income to provide the basics in life, such as food, clothing, and shelter. This inability is usually due to disease, disability, inadequate general education, and blocked opportunities. The emergence of the postindustrial state with its need for highly skilled employees further contributes to the problem as membership in the permanent underclass increases.

Poverty compounds other problems. The lifestyles associated with a constant struggle for survival often lead to broken homes, dysfunctional families, inadequate schooling, and ineffectual parenting. Divorce, abandonment, parental incarceration, domestic violence, substance abuse, and crime too often mark the lives of the poor.

Youth violence among the poor may appear in any of several guises. First there is violence associated with staying alive. Some youngsters steal, rob, and embezzle to obtain the basics in life that cannot be obtained by other more socially adaptive methods because these young people lack those more adaptive skills. Some accept fighting as a normal way in life to solve conflicts. Others turn to violence to earn a living. Selling drugs and other stolen property, shoplifting, hijacking cars, and prostitution are all methods of self-employment in the absence of formal education or training. Violence may also arise from witnessing domestic violence, from joining violent youth gangs, and from carrying weapons as a means of self-defense. The mean streets of poverty sometimes become armed camps in pursuit of the illusion of safety.

Domestic Violence

Domestic violence is the committing of violent acts against one's family and loved ones. Such violence includes physical abuse of one's spouse, children, stepchildren, or other distant relatives; sexual abuse of one's mate, children, or stepchildren; nonverbal intimidation to frighten or threaten family members by noninterpersonal acts and behaviors (e.g., stalking); verbal threats of intent to harm or denigrate; and acts of homicide committed against family members.

The physical abuse seen by those who work in emergency rooms includes knives, guns, baseball bats, high-heeled shoes, ashtrays, lit cigarettes, scissors, cards, ropes, doorknobs, hair brushes, bricks, acid, scalding water, motor vehicles, anything handy. Sexual abuse may include sadomasochistic acts, forced group sex, foreign objects being inserted into the vagina, forced sex with animals, and the use of cattle prods (Stacey and Shupe, 1983).

These acts of abuse are found in all age groups, both genders, all races, all ethnic groups, and all social classes.

As we noted earlier, many children who are direct victims of, or witnesses to, such violence become angry and full of rage, and become batterers and criminals themselves. Others become depressed, and turn this anger against themselves in the form of suicide.

Discrimination

Discrimination forms the basis for acts of hatred committed against innocent people who are singled out because of some aspect of their person. Race, ethnicity, religious beliefs, sexual preference, age, gender, and medical or psychiatric disability are its most common forms.

Furthermore, these citizens find themselves frequently excluded from equal opportunities in employment, housing, education, and other basic civil rights. At times, the laws and institutions of our society do not provide justice, respect, and equal opportunity for everyone.

Affluence. A beneficial economy may also be associated with you
violence. Many families have two wage earners, and many of th
have two jobs each. Much of this is driven by the postindustrial va
of the pursuit of material goods, and parents experience less time a
more stress as they compete for the good life. In these circumstanc
parents also have less time for their children, and television becon
the new baby-sitter for a generation of youngsters.

Affluence, ironically like poverty, comes with its own painful l
acy of divorce, substance abuse, domestic violence, and credit c
debt, the leading cause of marital breakup in our country. Neglec
children from affluent families also express their anger through ph
ical violence. Increases in suicides, date violence, destruction
property, bullying, robberies, wanton vandalism, addictions
drugs, and the homicides of one's peers suggest that the natio
pursuit of material goods is not adequately meeting the needs
affluent youth.

Inadequate Schooling

Schools provide a community outside of the home to reinforce
educational building blocks put in place by parents. Schools
serve to develop the values of the culture, and to foster tolera
self-discipline, delay of gratification, and character development

In many schools, however, these basic goals are thwarted by
teriorating physical plants, inadequate basic supplies, the absenc
computers, no national standards, and, in some school syste
even the absence of a teacher for each classroom. In addition,
instructional time provided by teachers is further limited as teac
are expected to be police officers, nurses, counselors, and pare
surrogates. Education is thus compromised at a time when
needed most.

Academic failure may be related to youth violence in at least
important ways. First, a lack of education may relegate one to
permanent underclass and a possible life of crime as a way of e
ing a living. Second, youngsters who feel academically inferior (
out of school, and frequently join gangs and the violence of li
the streets.

Violence breeds in this discontent. Those who are discriminated against may also find themselves the victims of violence by young people whose hate crimes may include murder, torture, arson, robbery, assault, rape, derogatory speech, and graffiti. Young people who feel left out of the mainstream of society use these acts to exact revenge on the adult world or to give themselves the illusion of power.

Another equally sad way in which victims of discrimination are exposed to violence is through aggression by their own youth. Unable to confront the large social ills, these young people vent their anger and sense of helplessness on their own disenfranchised group.

Substance Abuse/Easily Available Weapons

Substance abuse, including alcohol, is widespread in our society as a way of attaining instant gratification, and as a method of self-medicating the intense life stress associated with the emerging post-industrial state. Substance abuse may also be a way to earn a living.

Substance abuse is found in parents, teachers, counselors, managers, government leaders, ministers, doctors, police, and many others, including a large segment of our youth. In the emergency room of one hospital where I worked, we detoxified children as young as twelve years old. One has to drink a lot of alcohol for a length of time to develop an addiction at such a young age, but some of our young people have reached this point.

The presence of these foreign substances leads to clouded judgment and impulsive behavior that results in homicides, assaults, and armed robberies. This violence is further compounded by the drug trade where turf wars between drug dealers lead to street violence, including drive-by shootings of rivals and the enforcement of debt collection from buyers, who in turn commit crimes to support their habits (Goldstein, 1994).

Easily available weapons are employed for material gain, to eliminate witnesses, to convince the skeptical, to frighten the innocent, and to enhance self-esteem.

Gangs

Most adolescents chum around together in groups. Groups provide acceptance, peer approval, a sense of empowerment, a forum to learn new social skills, and sometimes relief from boredom. However, when the group turns to violence, the socialization processes are inherently corrupted.

Sociologist Carl Taylor (Prothrow-Stith, 1991) has written at length about three types of male gangs. Scavenger gangs are first, and are loosely organized groups with low achievers. Leadership changes often, and the group has no clear long-term goals. The second type of group is the territorial gang. These gangs fight to preserve geographical territory, usually have initiation rites that entail violence, and are formed by youth from troubled families. Corporate gangs form the third type of male groups. The reason for their existence is economic, not social. These groups are highly disciplined, have strong codes of behavior and secrecy, and are highly structured business units that usually sell drugs for profit.

To these male gangs can be added two types of girl gangs. Auxiliary girl gangs are linked to a male turf or corporate gang, and support the activities of their male peers. Independent girl gangs are themselves involved in turf issues or business opportunities apart from any specific male group.

Both male and female gangs are involved in some of our most brutal youth violence from initiation rites that can include murder to armed robberies, drive-by shootings, and vicious assaults that include torture and dismemberment of victims.

The Media

Although newspapers, radio, and television can be sources of information and cultural appreciation, for many of our youth it is the media that fosters drug usage, sexual promiscuity, and wanton violence and destruction. Through visual image and lyric, many of our youth are exposed to almost constant messages of destructive behavior. Often, there is no adult present to limit this viewing or interpret the negative aspects of these messages.

Thus, it is not surprising that research has shown that youngsters who are exposed to these media messages behave more aggressively. However, the relationship between media violence and a range of violent behaviors by young people (Wekesser, 1995) is complicated by other factors. Not all children who watch or listen to this programming become violent, and, when these programs are aired in other countries, the youth of those countries do not necessarily become violent.

Children respond in different ways to media violence. Some become frightened, some withdraw, some fictionalize, and some become violent. In this last category, the child has identified with the aggressor for some particular reason in the youngster's life. Victimizations at home or at school are possible precipitants in this identification with the aggressor, but a full understanding of the predisposing factor(s) is not presently known.

Psychological Factors

Psychological factors have typically focused on two spheres: reasonable mastery and a purposeful meaning in life. Reasonable mastery refers to our ability to shape our environment to meet our needs through our academic and interpersonal skills. A meaningful purpose in life provides us with a reason to be involved in the world about us. Problems in either of these areas in children and teenagers may result in important problems in development.

Faulty Mastery

A youngster's range of coping skills includes abilities needed to address the normal problems of everyday life such as managing life stress, finances, and time constraints; interpersonal skills needed for cooperative behavior with others to meet one's general goals; and academic achievement to have a basic understanding of how the world operates and to ensure the skills necessary to obtain employment in today's postindustrial knowledge-based society.

Failure to develop normally in any of these three areas may result in problem-solving deficits that compromise obtaining adequate in-

TABLE 2

Common Psychological Values and Attitudes in Youth Violence:

Catharsis
Excitement
Acceptance
Status
Self-Esteem
Seeking Justice
Revenge
Jealousy
Shame

---

come, as well as the ability to live comfortably in a community with others. These failures are often accompanied by feeling states that include anger, frustration, rejection, and aloneness, and problems with delay of gratification.

All of these factors have been associated with instances of crime by young people. Lack of schooling leads to less socially acceptable ways of earning a living, especially in the drug trade. The feeling states that we noted lead to abrasive interpersonal encounters that are replete with threats and actual violence toward others and property. Children without a reasonable complement of normal coping skills for addressing life stress are at high risk to become violent.

Faulty Meaning

Just as there are poor mastery skills, there is a set of values and attitudes about life that can create meaning in the young person's life that may lead to angry outbursts.

Table 2 presents some of the more common ones in today's age. Instead of values that might draw the child closer to the social fabric with others, these values and attitudes tend to create conflict among people that often result in violence and crime.

Catharsis is the need to express overwhelming feeling states of anger, frustration, sadness, and grief. In many young children, these expressions are not channeled in a restrained manner. Instead, they become free-floating, diffuse expressions of feelings that may result in damage to person or property. Control in these situations is tenuous or absent, and may be further complicated by the presence of drugs.

Excitement is another attitude that motivates much youthful behavior. For those with limited skills, planning is not for future success but rather immediate ways to relieve boredom in the here and now. This response to boredom can range from random acts of vandalism to the planning, implementation, and confrontation of serious crime such as armed robbery.

Acceptance is another common factor in youth violence. Peer approval is a powerful motivator, especially in teenagers. If the more normal channels for social acceptance are blocked, some youths will join gangs for acceptance, and these gangs provide many opportunities for youth violence to be displayed as a badge of membership and acceptance.

Some young people commit violent acts to gain status and dominance over their peer group. Often, the most violent males emerge as the group's leaders with all of the accoutrements of power, including choice of drugs, young females, motor vehicles, and a variety of other material goods. Closely related to dominance is the use of violence to express self-esteem. For those who feel helpless in the face of traditional cultural opportunities, who feel rejected by others, or who perceive themselves to be failures, violence is a powerful force for self-affirmation, i.e., a method of letting the adult world know that it needs to pay attention to the individual.

Seeking justice and seeking revenge are both methods of settling old scores by force. In the first case, the young person makes him- or herself judge and jury in righting some perceived injustice. In the second case, there is no pretense of justice, the youngster is exacting punishment for what the child perceives to be mistreatment.

Jealousy and shame are the last two powerful motivators in table 2. Jealousy arises when an individual wants something, but believes him- or herself helpless to obtain it. Jealousy motivates much girl violence when some girls are angered that other girls may prize a boyfriend, fancy clothes, or a better education. Shame is a state of embarrassment and, in some cases, self-hatred. Some of our young people have histories of severe physical or sexual abuse. They view themselves as damaged goods that are worthless and as persons who need to be punished for the abuse events that have left them disgraced. Violent behavior is one way to be caught and punished, not only for the immediate violent act, but as a deserved outcome for earlier transgressions for which they blame themselves.

Disruptions in reasonable mastery and meaning are continuously associated with being risk factors for violence in young people.

The Anomic Cycle of Violence

The various risk factors for youth violence are presented in summary form in table 3. This overview demonstrates why it is difficult to predict violence. There are many factors, and, more frequently, several are involved in any particular episode. Each individual case needs to be examined in detail.

Since no one can predict violence with one hundred percent accuracy, as we have noted, the better solution is to have a basic understanding of how these risk factors increase the probability of violence in any particular child, and to develop strategies to prevent these risk factors from asserting their deadly impact.

Is there any general way to understand these various factors that may help us in developing guidelines for prevention of youth violence? I believe there is, and I refer to it as the *anomic cycle of violence.*

The dramatic shift to the postindustrial state has created fertile ground for the lack of social cohesiveness. Add to this our cultural emphasis on the pursuit of material goods and many persons find themselves with less time, including less time for their children. Many of these children become frustrated, lonely, and angry, and often they feel rejected by the adult world. Some of these children then go on to become understandably depressed with a range of feelings from guilt and withdrawal to rage against others and rage against the self. If substance abuse, easily available weapons, and media models of violence are added to the equation, then the adult

TABLE 3

Possible Risk Factors in Youth Violence:

Biological	Risk	Sociological	Risk	Psychological	Risk
The Nervous System Genetics/ Instinct	No	*Inadequate Attachments:*	Yes	*Inadequate Mastery:*	
Temperament	Yes	Poverty/ Affluence	Yes	Personal Growth	Yes
Cortex	Yes	Inadequate Schooling	Yes	Interpersonal	Yes
Limbic System	Yes	Discrimination	Yes	Academic	Yes
Testosterone	No	Domestic Violence	Yes		
Medical Conditions	Yes	Substance Abuse/ Available Weapons	Yes	*Inadequate Meaning:*	
Psychiatric Conditions	Yes	Youth Gangs	Yes	Values/Attitudes	Yes
Personality Disorders	Yes	The Media	Yes		

community has a fundamental and general way of understanding much of the violence perpetrated by our young.

Although this anomic cycle of violence is not meant to predict specific acts of youth violence, it may serve as a helpful way of integrating the various risk factors of violence, so that caring adults have a general sense of how to understand the forces of aggression that are unleashed in the present age and how to highlight important areas for prevention. For example, rearing children is time, labor, and financially intensive. The adult community can ask if the society as a whole is leaving enough time for the complex task of child rearing. They can reflect on the importance of other people in their lives and the need for children to have similar ongoing caring attachments. Similarly, parents and other adults may want to consider addressing substance abuse, childhood depression, and the like.

The emergence of the postindustrial shift cannot be stopped, but the anomic conditions that it creates in our youth can be addressed. By identifying these risk factors early on, much of the youth violence that now confronts us can be prevented.

This completes our review of youth violence and its many causes. Our inquiry in part 1 has examined the array of violent crimes committed by today's youth, crimes committed by children and adolescents of both genders, all social classes, and all races. These crimes are being committed by our young people in our neighborhoods, in our schools, and even in our own homes. While it is true that there have been recent modest declines in this violence, the overall extent of youth violence remains a grim reality.

Equally extensive has been our discussion of the theories of youth violence. There is no single factor that can predict youth violence because its causes are many and varied. However, with the exception of severe medical or psychiatric conditions in some rare cases, violent young people are not out of their minds. They are conscious of the manner in which they are venting the full extent of their rage on society. The depraved indifference of many of them is truly frightening.

Since our goal is to prevent violence in the first place, part 2 of this book looks at the continuum of warning signs, warning signs in many of our children and teenagers that lead to the causes of violence that have been reviewed in this chapter. The emphasis in part 2 is on identifying the warning signs of trouble so that remedial strategies may be employed before the causes of violence erupt. These signs include, in order of severity, **(1) the early warning signs** associated with developmental disruptions in the basic domains of reasonable mastery, caring attachments to others, and a meaningful purpose in life; (2) **the serious warning signs** of untreated depression, substance abuse, and PTSD; and (3) **the urgent warning signs** associated with conduct disorder, the precursor to adult criminal violence.

We turn first to the early warning signs.

PART TWO

YOUTH VIOLENCE:
THE WARNING SIGNS

Dateline: Chicago. August 31, 1994.

It began quietly enough in 1983 in one of Chicago's many hospitals. A young boy, who would be later known as "Yummy" because of his fondness for cookies and candy bars, was born into the world and took up residence on the city's South Side. The promise of his future was, of course, unknown at the time.

Yummy's childhood was not typical for most children. He was seen at a local hospital at age twenty-two months for scratches on his neck and bruises on his arms and torso. A year later, additional scars on his face, many cordlike marks on his abdomen, and cigarette burns on various places on his body led authorities to send him on an itinerant's journey from foster homes to other social service institutions.

His preteen years were not typical either. A childhood of knives, guns, and fire setting were linked in his adolescence to stealing cars, selling drugs, and extorting monies. In all, he had a juvenile record of twenty-three felonies and eight misdemeanors.

In a neighborhood where a twenty-year-old qualified as a senior citizen, Yummy significantly increased his risk of dying young when he joined the Black Disciples gang.

On August 28, 1994, armed with a nine millimeter semiautomatic weapon, he was sent by the Disciples to kill a rival gang member over some perceived gang shortcoming. Yummy missed the rival, and killed an innocent fourteen-year-old girl who was standing in her yard at a family barbecue.

His brother Disciples were afraid that Yummy would talk to the police.

Thus, on August 31, 1994, in the darkness of the marble tunnel that formed a railway viaduct, the four-foot-eight-inch, sixty-eight pound, eleven-year-old killer met his end. His lifeless body stilled by two bullets in the back of his head, execution style. His blood trickling in the mud.

The hunter had become the prey.

The late Thomas Dooley, M.D., a medical humanitarian who worked among the peoples of Southeast Asia, once observed that, if you use the weapon of hate, you will get hatred for a response. Here is a clear example of how hatred in early childhood returned as terror for a neighborhood a decade later. An eleven-year-old killer garners little sympathy, but he was a child and his bleak life circumstances may help us to reflect on what we can do to prevent similar cases of this type of youth violence. Here are some questions to guide our inquiry in part 2:

1. Could this child and others like him have been helped early on to prevent their violent acts?
2. Were there any warning signs of possible impending violence?
3. How could one recognize these signs?
4. Are some of these signs more serious than others?
5. If there is more than a single warning sign, where does one begin?

3

EARLY WARNING SIGNS: DISRUPTIONS IN MASTERY, ATTACHMENTS, AND MEANING

There is a destiny that makes us brothers.
None goes his way alone.
—Oliver Wendell Holmes

A man's character is his fate.
—Heraclitus

"I hate that bitch."

Laurel voiced the sentiment for both herself and her fellow sixteen-year-old companion, Marianne.

Patricia, a young fifteen-year-old girl who was the focus of this rage, was a quiet, shy, self-effacing teenager, who was plain in appearance and of modest normal intelligence. Her two goals in life were to obtain a college education as her parents wished, and to find a boyfriend who would be hers forever. She knew that she was not pretty, but she hoped that loyalty, hard work, and a college education would somehow compensate. Because school work was so hard for her, she studied for long hours into the night. However, each evening just before bedtime, in the quiet darkness she asked God to please bring her someone to love.

Although Laurel and Marianne would have nothing to do with school work themselves, they did resent Patricia's efforts to better herself.

"How dare she try to be different?"

Their jealous minds would have none of it. She needed to be taught a lesson that she would never forget.

On the first Friday afternoon of April, they waited at the corner of Mandrake and Pells Avenue for Patricia's returning school bus. As the bus pulled away, Laurel and Marianne rushed Patricia, knocked her to the ground, and slashed her facial cheeks mercilessly with two box cutters.

"Take that, you bitch. No guy would want you anyway. You're ugly. These scars will help you remember that."

In the quiet efficiency of the emergency room, fifty-seven stitches later, Patricia cried silently, and confronted her great lonely ache.

"Why me? Whatever did I do? Who could love me now?"

How can this be? Here is a young teenage girl with the basic dreams of many teenage girls, following her parents' directives, working hard, avoiding trouble. Yet two embittered, jealous young girls in a suburban high school with lives that are going nowhere strike out in rage at an innocent bystander. Where was the adult community? Were there no warning signs for parents, teachers, and counselors?

In this chapter, the focus is on the three domains associated with good physical and mental health (Flannery, 1994a, 1994b): reasonable mastery, caring attachments to others, and a meaningful purpose in life.

As was noted in passing in the previous chapter, reasonable mastery refers to our abilities to shape the world in socially acceptable ways to meet our needs. Formal education, life experiences, and observing others provide us with solutions for getting our needs met. The concept of reasonableness is important because not all of life's problems are solvable by any given individual, and part of mastery skills is in knowing when a problem cannot be solved. The term caring attachments refers to those other persons who are close to us. Included are family, friends, classmates, colleagues at work, and the like. These significant other people help us through the ups and downs of life as our companions on life's journey. A meaningful purpose in life is our reason to live, and includes any persons or projects that motivates us to invest our energy in the world each day.

Good mastery, attachments, and meaning emerge over time in the process of normal childhood and adolescent growth. Disruptions in these normal developmental processes provide the early warning signs of potential trouble, including violence. Somewhere in the lives of Laurel and Marianne something went amiss. Perhaps attachments were ruptured by divorce, perhaps a learning disability interfered with academics, perhaps personal incest made life seem senseless. The vignette does not provide us this information, but somewhere a fundamental flaw occurred, and the warning signs, such as disinterest in school, went unheeded. The scarred face of a young teenage girl is painful testimony to the violent rage that finally erupted.

Children and adolescents, whose early messages of distress are not understood or are ignored, may become depressed and suicidal; they may abuse alcohol or drugs in attempts to self-medicate their states of psychological distress; or they may withdraw from active participation in the world if they have been victims of violence and are experiencing PTSD. These behaviors comprise the second set of warning signs, the serious warning signs. Like the early warning signs, the serious warning signs also have many signals of distress, and, like the early warning signs, if left untreated, violence against the self or others may follow.

The third and most urgent warning signs are those associated with conduct disorder. Here, there have been warning signs for many years as youngsters became increasingly involved in trouble, both in terms of frequency and severity. Again, if the urgent warning signs are not heeded, these troubled young people will progress toward serious violence against person and property, and an adult life of crime and violence will most likely follow.

It need not be this way. The adult community can learn to identify the various sets of warning signs, can learn to understand what has gone amiss, and can learn to identify the resources needed to address the problem before further suffering occurs. However, no parent, teacher, or counselor is expected to be able to solve every child's problem. Rather, the goal here is to identify the warning signs, and to steer the child to the needed resources. The resource person may or may not be the individual who first identified the warning sign or problem.

Of the early warning signs, caring attachments are the most fundamental. These attachments sustain us, teach us the mastery skills that we need in order to survive, and provide powerful meanings for daily life.

We begin with an infant in tears.

Caring Attachments

The Nature of Attachments

This scene is familiar to all of us. The baby is in its mother's arms. It is quiet and contented as it explores the world around it with its eyes and little hands. Suddenly, the mother puts the child down to complete another task. The baby howls, shrieks, and cries continuously and intensely. Its little body trembles in frantic, chaotic movements, until the mother returns to calm and soothe the child.

A noisy initiation for family and friends, but of importance in the child's life, because the child knows at some level of awareness that without the primary care giver he or she will literally die.

This linkage, or attachment, between the child and the birth mother, or other primary caretaker such as foster mother, adoptive mother, or father, is known as *bonding*. It begins at birth and provides the infant with both protection from predators and a teacher of the skills needed to ensure survival.

The importance of the bonding process has been studied at length by psychiatrist John Bowlby (1973). Dr. Bowlby noticed three stages of distress in children separated from their parents or other primary care givers. The first stage is the frantic searching that has just been described. This is followed by a state of despair and depression, if the parent does not return. This, in turn, is followed by a state of detachment in which the child withdraws from the world in order to prevent being abandoned again. Many of the warning signs to be outlined here in part 2 have disrupted attachments at their core, and are found in children and teenagers who are angry, depressed, or withdrawn.

Recently, Masten and Coatsworth (1998) have shown the process of bonding also to be important in the child's development of self-regulation in the areas of attention, emotion, and behavior. Ongoing interactions with the mother develop these rudimentary skills as the mother directs the child's attention to new objects, soothes the distress of the child, or teaches the child skills, such as walking and speaking. The development of these skills has been shown to result in prosocial behaviors, peer acceptance, better problem-solving skills, and good academic performance. Children who are not taught this regulatory process have more antisocial behavior, peer rejection, and academic difficulties.

When the attachment process is present on an ongoing basis, the outcome is a young adult who is productive for him- or herself and for society. When the attachment process is disrupted, premature death, violence against the self, and violence against others are often the result.

Some of the more important forms of these disruptions that may lead to violence have already been noted. Durkheim's work on disruptions in the social fabric led to increases in suicide and substance abuse, and the biological problems of reactive attachment disorder, oppositional defiant disorder, and conduct disorder are all associated with disruptions in early attachments. Each of the sociological factors (poverty/affluence, inadequate schooling, discrimination, domestic violence, substance abuse/available weapons, youth gangs, and the technological isolation of the media) are also associated with disruptions in caring attachments between peoples, and, as we have seen, each factor is related to a variety of different types of violence by our young people.

Our overview of caring attachments continues by enumerating some of the more important interpersonal skills that parents and primary care givers teach to their children, skills that reduce the likelihood of violence later in the youth's life.

Fostering Attachments

1. *Trust.* The constant presence of the primary care giver in addressing the needs of the child teaches the child that the world is a safe place where people can be trusted. This process fosters the growth of a sense of trust.

Trust has two fundamental components: predictable behavior and similar values. In order for one person to trust another, the other person's behavior must be reasonably predictable in most cases. What a person says he or she will do must be commensurate with how he or she actually behaves. While the complexity of the world gives us some leeway for occasional mismatches (e.g., being late because of unexpected traffic delays), the presence of sporadic, random, or inconsistent behavior on the part of the other party precludes the formation of trust.

If predictable behavior is present, then the development of trust involves a second step, that of assessing whether both parties have generally similar values. If one believes in hard work, sexual exclusivity, and reasonable money management, and the other believes in loafing, promiscuity, and gambling, trust is unlikely to emerge. Even though the behavior may be predictable (e.g., the other party will gamble each week), the value systems are too dissimilar to permit the development of trust.

Children who grow up in homes marked by harsh and erratic discipline, parental substance abuse, parental physical abuse, and abandonment are not likely to develop trust. Instead, they often develop a mind-set of jungle survival: trust no one. Watch out for yourself. Attack them before they attack you.

2. *Empathy.* Empathy is the ability to understand how another person is experiencing an event. It is the ability to step into another person's shoes, as it were, to understand that person's view of an event. The capacity for empathy is important in problem solving where different individuals may have differing feelings about a situation.

Children are taught to be empathic by their parents and other caring adults. It often is learned by trying to understand how a pet may feel if it is injured, or what might be the reasons that a younger sibling is crying. The child learns that others have feelings about events that may differ from the child's, or feelings that may have resulted from the child's own behavior. Empathy covers the range of feelings from joy to depressed grief, and prepares the child for peer and other social groups outside of the home.

We have a number of young people now who murder other young people. They apparently are not disturbed at taking human life in part because they have not learned to be empathic.

3. *Sharing*. Closely related to empathy is the ability to share resources and accept responsibilities in cooperative efforts with others. Mothers set the foundation for sharing during the early self-regulatory process by encouraging the child to share with siblings and friends, to do household chores, and to take care of pets. Just as all family members benefit from various rewards, so each has a responsibility to work for the common good of all its members. These initial skills become reinforced by school and peer group experiences, and result in children and adolescents who behave responsibly and do not resort to violence to have their own way.

4. *Grieving*. All life involves loss. Loss of loved ones, loss of property, and loss of wished-for goals are some of its more common manifestations. Grieving is the process by which humans come to terms with each loss and move on in life. Children who are unable to grieve remain depressed, and may become violent toward themselves in the form of suicide.

There are five stages in the grieving process (Kübler-Ross, 1969). The first stage is that of denial, a moment in which the fact of the loss is not comprehended or accepted. No one died, thinks the child. The second stage of anger reflects the individual's unwillingness to accept the finality of the loss. It's not fair that my mother died, thinks the grieving child. Bargaining comes next, and reflects the individual's wish not to accept the full finality as yet. Perhaps my mother can live until my fifth birthday, muses the child. The fourth stage is that of depression when the full impact and weight of the loss is understood. In time this passes, and the individual accepts that the event is over, and begins to construct a new life without the lost person or material object.

5. *Self-Esteem*. Self-esteem is the process by which we evaluate our strengths and weaknesses so that we have some comprehensive sense of our personhood. While all of us have weaknesses, a true evaluation of our strengths in the face of our limitations provides us with needed self-assurance throughout life, especially in life's more difficult moments.

A key factor in this process is an accurate assessment of both true strengths and true weaknesses. An excessive emphasis on strengths, and perceived, but not true, successes may result in narcissism and arrogance. An excessive emphasis on weaknesses, and perceived, but not true, failures may result in chronic depression.

The most helpful approach for developing good self-esteem is to help the child evaluate each of its activities. Little Johnny washed his hands, put away his toys, and took his nap when he was asked to. These are all positive. However, little Johnny did not feed his pet and pushed his little sister. These are not acceptable behaviors, and reflect weaknesses that need further correction. Statements without reference to specific behaviors are usually not helpful. Statements such as "you are a bad boy" or "you are just like your mother" are confusing to a child, are not accurate, and will not assist the child in developing adequate self-esteem. This process of evaluating specific events over time will help the child to develop a true sense of self, and, as the child learns better skills, the youngster's self-esteem will increase.

Good self-esteem keeps children from resorting to violence in the face of failure, rejection by others, or loss.

Disruptions in Attachments

Table 1 outlines some of the more common disruptions in attachments that face many of our youth in all social classes. Each of these has been associated with violence in some youths.

First are disruptions to bonds within the family itself. These include divorce, separation, desertion, nonsupport, single parenting, and foster care placements. In each of these situations, children lose the presence of at least one caring biological parent, and these matters need to be considered seriously.

For example, there are many divorces in our culture, and it is true that some marriages are violent and unworkable and the children are better off removed from the situation. However, routine divorce needs to be balanced against its impact on children. Children of divorced parents are known to be at increased risk for substance abuse, depression, and violence toward self or others (e.g., see Wallerstein and Blakeslee [1989]). The other examples of disrupted attachments within the family unit are also associated with serious negative impacts on the couple's children.

TABLE 1

Disruptions in Attachments:

Disrupted Family Unit	Divorce, Separation, Desertion, Nonsupport, Single Parent, Foster Care
Dysfunctional Family Unit	Physical or Sexual Abuse, Verbal Threats, Substance Abuse, Gambling, Severe Financial Debt, Unemployment, Social Isolation

Absence of Peer Group

Disrupted Relationships at School and in the Neighborhood

Although dysfunctional family units may stay together, a second category of disrupted attachments arises from the dysfunctional issues within the family unit. Physical or sexual abuse, severe verbal threats, substance abuse, gambling, severe financial debt, long-term unemployment, and severe social isolation are all associated with enhanced life stress. This additional life stress sometimes results in increased arguing and in some cases pushing, shoving, or other forms of violence or aggression.

Consider another example. In a society that values the accumulation of material goods, this lifestyle is often financed by credit card debt. Many people do not realize that credit card debt is the leading cause of divorce in our country, and that many children witness physical abuse between their parents in the course of the divorce proceedings. Similarly, other unaddressed dysfunctional family issues lead to angry children who exact revenge on others or themselves.

The final grouping of disruptions in attachments occur outside of the home. These include disruptions in attachments to peers, disruptions that occur in school with teachers and classmates, and disruptions that occur among neighbors in a community. A common cause in many of these disruptions is violence by other youths, a situation that precludes the development of more normal caring attachments.

Reasonable Mastery

The Nature of Mastery

Since reasonable mastery involves developing the skills to shape our environment, by definition it is a lengthy process. It includes the three fundamental areas of general concern already noted: personal growth skills, interpersonal skills, and academic skills. Let us start with a brief description of how the child's brain processes information, when it is developing thinking, feelings, and behaviors. This will help us understand the normal developmental processes that children go through when they learn mastery skills, and it may also help us identify some of the root problems of the warning signs when things go awry.

The first step in this process is known as perception. The child's sense receptors of vision, hearing, smell, taste, and the like gather information about the environment at a given point in time. This information passes through the body's nerve fibers, across the synaptic gaps of these nerve fibers, and on into the brain where these nerve impulses of information pass through the limbic system into the cortex. When this information is in the cortex, the brain scans past memory for similar events, compares these past memories with current experience, and develops some possible plans of action. This step is known as cognition. Perceptions and cognitions are organized into categories of importance so that an individual need not pay full attention to every event.

The child learns basic values and attitudes as it interacts with the environment. Values are fundamental principles of desirable courses of action, and attitudes are beliefs that are formed in interactions with events around us. Some examples: One parent may teach a child to value the welfare of others; another parent, to value material goods. One child may play with an animal and enjoy it, and develop the attitude that pets are fine. Another child may be bitten by an animal and conclude that pets are dangerous. Values and attitudes may be learned from parents, other family members, clergy, teachers, peers, neighbors, or from the child's own personal life experiences.

When this process of perception, cognition, values, and attitudes leads to productive, socially sanctioned responses, the results are adaptive and helpful to the child and society. However, if the steps in the process are not productive and socially acceptable and the child does not have the necessary coping skills, violence may be one negative outcome. Antisocial values and attitudes may shape a child's response to the world and the people in it. Selfishness, hatred, and intense anger over failure or being rejected are all values and attitudes that have led young people to commit violence against other youngsters.

For these reasons, it is important to instill in children reasonable mastery skills that are prosocial, and adaptive for both the child and the world it lives in.

Fostering Reasonable Mastery

There are obviously many basic skills that parents teach their children over time. Some common areas that have been shown to be adaptive are noted below.

1. Personal Growth Skills. Stress management skills in the broadest sense are an important component in today's child rearing. Children are easily overwhelmed by the fast pace of the postindustrial state and the intense emphasis on competitiveness for success. This needs to be counterbalanced with physical exercise, relaxation exercises of some form, a sensible diet, and time for play. Play is not wasted time. It provides children with an opportunity to practice new skills before the performance of those skills becomes a matter of evaluation. Children also need to be taught not to resort to drugs or alcohol as a way of reducing stress, or of altering brain perception as a way of escaping from reality. Stress management techniques will give children and teenagers the needed adaptive skills for coping with the stress of life in our current age.

Time and money management are also important skills in preventing possible aggressive outbursts. Just as overstressed children may act out their rage toward others or take their own lives to escape the pressure, children who believe that they have too much to do or are in severe credit card debt are similar high risk candidates to act impulsively in anger. The child may in fact have too much to do, and parental and teacher help in setting priorities and reasonable limits may be of great assistance. Similarly, basic education about income, banking, and debt in a capitalist system may free a child from endless hours of frustration in a society that stresses material acquisition.

Media literacy is another important area for personal growth in our information-based society. Children spend long hours interacting with television, the world wide web, current music programming, and other media. They are exposed to visual messages, lyrics, and written information that stimulates them, that is often something that they have not experienced, and that does not spell out the long-term implications of the message. For example, teenagers are targeted with messages about the glamour of smoking, but rarely about its deadly health consequences. Frequently, the media uses violence and sex to draw children's attention. Parents, teachers, and other adults interested in children need to explore these media messages with children, so that the children understand the risks and long-term outcomes. In this process, children may also be taught what might be more socially acceptable outcomes to the issues raised by the various media.

While these may not be the first personal growth skills that a parent might consider, it is becoming increasingly evident that lack of mastery in these areas leads to aggressive outbursts in many children in today's age.

2. *Interpersonal Growth.* Again, there are many tasks that parents will want to teach their children about how to get along with others. This section is not meant to overwhelm already busy parents and teachers, but rather to highlight where focused efforts may have the best possibility of reducing youth violence.

Interpersonal growth centers on how the child will interact with others so that the needs of both parties are reasonably addressed.

Some of these skills such as trust, empathy, acceptance of others, and sharing overlap with the development of caring attachments. Additional interpersonal skills, however, may prove to enhance greatly the child's quality of life.

Learning to identify one's mood states correctly is one important skill. Recognizing anger, frustration, depression, and the like, and dealing with these dysphoric states without resorting to guns or some other form of violence is an important mastery skill.

Developing good problem-solving skills supplements the correct identification of mood states. Verbal conflict resolution, developing a range of alternative solutions for any given problem, learning to negotiate and compromise are prosocial adaptive solutions that decrease the probability of violence.

Children need to learn personal responsibility and self-discipline, so that they can tolerate frustration and delay of gratification. Simple tasks early on, such as saving one's allowance for two weeks for a more expensive meal out, are basic ways to teach self-discipline. The examples are as varied as there are parents and teachers to construct them.

Children also need the experience of failing within a supportive context. None of us succeeds at everything we do, and a supportive context in the moment of failure demonstrates to the child that the child is not a failure as a person, that no one can do everything, and that one is still lovable in the face of life's defeats. Our culture of success frequently leaves our children who do not succeed at various tasks feeling like failures and outcasts. Often, they withdraw or strike back in anger.

3. Academic Growth. Formal education and training in the post-industrial state are critical for the child to foster the skills needed for success. Lesser levels of educational attainment may result in a poor quality of life, and even membership in the permanent underclass. For both the poor and the affluent, academic failure and inadequate coping strategies are associated with many types of crime and violence, as we have seen.

Children need to be computer literate. The computer has become a major force in commerce and in the research that leads to new advances in technology and health. Computers also permeate the service economy as any car mechanic working on computer timed engines can attest. Computers permeate the lives of all of us through credit cards, electronic reservation systems, and the delivery of food stuffs to the local grocery store. Mastering the essentials of the computer is a necessary component for today's high school graduate.

A second lesson from the computer is that reading skills are still very important in an age of television and other visual and aural media. Research findings, business opportunities, and financial transactions all take place in writing on computer screens and printouts. Children need to be proficient in reading, writing, composition, spelling, and arithmetic. Computer proficiency in the absence of basic literacy places the child at undue academic and economic risk.

As parents review their children's learning progress, parents will also want to instill in the child the concept of lifelong learning. The explosion of information in recent research from all four corners of the world will only continue to grow. Needed job skills and job opportunities will continue to evolve, and those children who have learned early on the importance of staying current will be in the most advantageous positions to succeed.

Another important consideration for many of today's parents in approaching the child's educational development is the role of child care. Child care serves two important purposes. It permits maternal employment and it may assist with the child's development. Day care settings range in type from care by other family relatives, to care in small groups in a neighbor's home, to placements in formal day-care program businesses. Staffing requirements and regulations vary greatly from state to state. The content and quality of what is taught also varies considerably so that parents need to evaluate their child's day program closely.

Child psychologist Sandra Scarr (1998) has recently reviewed the findings on child care. She found that the varying qualities of child care have only small effects on children's development, and that there is no known long-term impact from child care, except in the case of disadvantaged children who benefit from the intellectual and social experiences that might not be available to them at home.

Research in this area is new, and there may well be important effects that are not documented as yet. In the interim, parents will want to carefully evaluate the specific child-care situation that they have chosen to be sure that the child's intellectual, social, and emotional needs are being met. Since not all day-care programs may be strong in all areas, when parents are with their children, the parents can focus on those areas of additional needed development for any particular child that are not emphasized in the day-care program itself.

Disruptions in Reasonable Mastery

Disruptions in reasonable mastery may be identified by the absence of needed skills and faulty attitudes. Inadequate personal growth leads to children who are overwhelmed with life stress and are unable to manage either money or time effectively. Problems in interpersonal growth will manifest themselves in masked feelings, poor problem-solving skills, irresponsibility, poor cooperation, low frustration tolerance, and impulsivity. Academic failure is noted in poor grades, and in basic skill deficiencies in comprehension, the use of language, and basic deficits in common cultural information. Violence is a common outcome in many of the children and teenagers who lack these various skills.

Meaningful Purpose in Life

The Nature of Meaningfulness

All of us need a reason to guide our daily lives, a purpose that makes us invest our energy in the world around us, and that can help us in life's darker moments. Purposeful goals give a meaning to our lives and to those of our children.

Sociologist Aaron Antonovsky (1979) believes that a sense of coherence about the world is necessary for any individual to develop a true sense of purpose. In his view, three components are necessary for coherence to occur. The individual must find the world to be manageable so that the individual has some control over that environment. The person must also perceive the world as having some reasonable order and predictability so that the person can accurately comprehend the environment. Finally, the individual needs to believe that the world is worthy of investing his or her energies in it.

With a sense of coherence in place, children and adults are free to develop a variety of meaningful purposes. Our postindustrial state offers a variety of choices, including power, fame, recognition, social status, material gain, and instant celebrity. However, a second sociologist, the late Ernest Becker (1973), directs our attention to a more fundamental issue in human meaning making. Humans are both spiritual and biological. The spiritual self knows that the biological self will die, and seeks a way to find a transcendent meaning in life so that the spiritual self will live on in the memories of others after its death.

The values held out by the postindustrial state will not solve this problem as they all end with physical death. Becker's suggestion is to have meaningful goals that link us to others, that lead us to be concerned for the welfare of others, so that we can live on in the minds of others. Some examples might include creating a caring marriage, rearing children, teaching children, counseling children, or performing acts of personal charity. These other-centered goals are transcendent and are rooted in the memories of others, even as the individual may experience suffering, disability, and eventually death.

Fostering Meaningfulness

Children learn about values and meaning from direct instruction and from the behavior modeled by the adult community. They observe acts of charity and other concerns for the welfare of the human family, but they also observe cheating, corruption, substance abuse, selfishness, and violence. The development of transcendent prosocial meanings in children needs to be created and reinforced by parents, teachers, counselors, and other care givers. Many adults in today's age wisely look toward instilling in children the values of hard work, honesty, self-denial, and concern for others as ways to mitigate against the use of violence in resolving conflict.

Disruptions in Meaningfulness

Adults observe the absence of prosocial meaning in children when they see open disavowals of socially necessary values, the absence of any sense of guilt, and wanton disregard for others, all of which are associated with violence in youth.

Some of these disruptions are the end outcomes of poor child rearing practices. The published literature over the years has been remarkably consistent on the best practices for rearing children. Warmth, structure, clear rules, expectations for good behavior, both rewards and penalties, and a basic respect for the child have been associated with the growth of good children. On the other hand, when the child is not valued in the parents' lives, and discipline is harsh, punitive, rejecting, and inconsistent, violence and criminal behavior often follow.

The data appear clear. Children are happy and skilled when they are reared, educated, and counseled by adults in whom concern for the welfare of children has transcendent meaning.

Table 2 presents a summary overview of the early warning signs that are associated with disruptions in reasonable mastery, caring attachments to others, and a meaningful purpose in life. The biological markers from the previous chapter have been added in the interests of clarity, and for the purpose of having one central location for this informational guide. These early warning signs follow from basic disruptions in the normal developmental processes that we have reviewed, and each, when left unattended, may result in violence by young people.

In some instances the early warning signs are not recognized for what they are. In others, the potential for harm is minimized, and in some cases, it is suppressed (e.g., incest). When the early warning signs are left unattended, the disruptions fester, and their impact may result in a worsening of the child's condition. In addition, children with good growth and no disruptions may suddenly experience major disruptions in spite of all the good efforts of parents, teachers, and counselors. Becoming despondent over the loss of an opposite-sex friend, being lured by a peer group into experimenting with

TABLE 2

The Early Warning Signs:

I. Biological Illness	Injury to Cortex or Limbic System Temperament (Sensation-Seeking, Risk Taking, Impulsivity) Medical or Psychiatric Condition Personality Disorder
II. Attachments	Disrupted Family Unit: Divorce, Separation, Desertion, Nonsupport, Single Parent, Foster Care Dysfunctional Family Unit: Physical or Sexual Abuse, Verbal Threats, Substance Abuse, Gambling, Severe Financial Debt, Unemployment, Social Isolation Absence of Peer Groups Disrupted Relationships at School or in Neighborhood
III. Reasonable Mastery	Personal Growth: Overwhelmed by Life Stress, Unable to Manage Time or Finances Interpersonal Growth: Masked Feelings, Poor Problem-Solving Skills, Irresponsible, Low Frustration Tolerance, Impulsivity Academic Growth: Poor Grades, Deficiencies in Comprehension, Language, Cultural Information
IV. Meaningfulness	Disavows Prosocial Values, Disregard for Others

drugs, or being a victim of violence on neighborhood streets are all examples of how children who were doing well may suddenly be overwhelmed by painful life events.

When the early warning signs are not addressed, or when sudden life events overwhelm the child, the second set of warning signs may emerge. These are known as the serious warning signs because their potential negative impact for violence is greater than the early warning signs because they are more difficult to remedy. The next chapter considers in depth three of the more common serious warning signs: depression with potential suicide, substance abuse, and PTSD.

4

SERIOUS WARNING SIGNS: DEPRESSION, SUBSTANCE ABUSE, POSTTRAUMATIC STRESS DISORDER

Defeat strikes the young the hardest
because they least expect it.
—Abraham Lincoln

For in its innermost depths
youth is lonelier than old age.
—Anne Frank

Get it over with, jerk, she thought to herself.

When he was done, Michelle cleaned up, got dressed, and went back to the parlor to wait for her next customer. Two down, five to go.

She hated prostitution, but something within her that she did not understand drove her to do it. She was also feeding an expensive cocaine addiction, and seventeen-year-old high school dropouts didn't have many career options. The other girls thought she was crazy because she insisted beforehand that each of her customers never use the word *relax*. The word itself depressed her.

It had begun when she was six. Until that point, her childhood had been relatively happy and normal. She had friends, did well in school, and adored her puppy, whom she had named Faithful. This happiness ended when her father's gambling led to parental divorce, and her mother took Michelle and Faithful out of state.

The loneliness was terrible. It became even worse when her mother linked up with an alcoholic boyfriend named Larry. She was eight, when the reign of terror began. Larry began what would become his seven-year ritual of slipping into her room for sex. Each time, he held a butcher knife to her throat, and said "Relax or Faithful dies."

Years of forced oral, vaginal, and anal sex followed, but her heart was irrevocably broken forever when Larry forced her to have sex with Faithful. She ran away into the darkness on the very night that Faithful had finally died in his sleep.

Such was her life now. Medicating her depression with cocaine, forbidding the word *relax* to avoid those painful memories of the past, and earning a living by doing what she hated most....

"Forgive me, Faithful. I did love you. I didn't care about my own life, but I always feared for yours."

Do these things really happen to children? Sadly, they do. It is estimated that one child dies every six hours in our country from abuse or neglect at the hands of its parents. Add to this the data from our earlier review of violence inflicted on children by adults and other youths, and the nature of our national public health epidemic of violence becomes more clearly illustrated. Moreover, this gruesome violence is not occurring in isolated pockets here and there. It is found in all neighborhoods and in all social classes. Michelle was not a projects kid. She was from an upper-middle-class family with two professional parents before her father's gambling made a shambles of their attachments to one another. It is not surprising that such suffering leads young people to anger and to violence toward others or the self.

In this chapter, we turn our attention to the serious warning signs of the continuum of warning signs. These warning signs are serious because they are more immediately disruptive to the child's level of functioning, potentially more immediate in terms of violent behavior, and more immediate in terms of needed treatment. These serious warning signs may arise when early warning signs are dismissed, or, when overwhelming events occur in the lives of otherwise normal children, as we have noted. For example, in Michelle's case, the early warning signs of dysfunctional family gambling went unaddressed for several years. This led to another early warning sign in the disrupted attachments that followed in the wake of her parents' divorce. Apparently, the impact of the divorce also went unaddressed, and was followed by sexual abuse in the home. With the early warning signs ignored, by age seventeen, Michelle had developed the serious warning signs.

This chapter presents the three serious warning signs that are most common: depression, substance abuse, and PTSD. Michelle has been chosen as our example because she was struggling with all three of the serious warning signs. Her life illustrates a common outcome. It is not unusual for troubled youth to have two or more of the serious warning signs at the same time. The more warning signs that are left untreated, the greater is the likelihood that youth violence will erupt.

Our inquiry begins with depression and its frequent concomitant of suicidal thoughts and actions.

Depression

The Nature of Depression

All of us have been depressed at one time or another, and the child or adolescent's experience of depression is not all that different from that of parents, teachers, counselors, and other adults. The depressed young person is likely to encounter feelings of sadness, hopelessness, guilt, and depression. Tears, irritability, and loss of energy are common as is anhedonia, the absence of any pleasurable interest in activities of the world. In addition, the young person may have trouble concentrating and remembering at home and at school, and suicidal thoughts or plans may also be present.

Depressed young people may also experience disruptions in physical functioning. There may be loss of appetite, constipation, and alterations in the sleep cycle that might include lengthy hours of sleep or early morning awakening in a depressed or agitated state. Teenagers may experience a loss of interest in sex. Depression in younger children may be especially marked by anhedonia, mood irritability, and failures in meeting targeted weight gains.

TABLE 1

Depression: Some Possible Warning Signs:

Feelings	Sadness, Guilt, Hopelessness, Depression, Anhedonia, Irritability
	Sense of Worthlessness
Thinking	Problems with Concentration and Memory
	Suicidal Thoughts or Plans
Bodily States	Disruptions in Appetite, Sleep, Bowels, Libido

There are two main types of depression. One is known as major depressive episode, and the other as dysthymic disorder.

While both have many of the symptoms in table 1 in common, a major depressive episode is far more severe. A major depression generally interferes with the young person's functioning at home, at school, and with peers. In very severe cases, the young person may spend long hours isolated in his or her room. The physical disruptions are apt to be present, and the young person is at increased risk for suicidal thoughts and actions. Impairment from major depressive episodes may happen once in the person's life, or may recur at frequent intervals.

Dysthymic disorder is a chronic, less intense, less severe state of depressive functioning. Here the young adult is generally unhappy and blue, but is able to function to some degree at school and at home. The youngster remains irritable and generally less interested in the world, but physical disruptions in appetite, sleep, and the like are usually less severe, as is the risk of acute suicide. If left untreated, this dysthymic state may last several years.

At any given point in time, the prevalence of a major depressive episode in the general population for children is 0.4-2.5 percent and 0.4-8.3 percent for adolescents. The prevalence for dysthymic disorder in children is 0.6-1.7 percent and 1.6-8.0 percent for teenagers (Cicchetti and Toth, 1998). Seventy to eighty percent of adolescent depression is not adequately treated, and in many cases the depression is made worse by the adolescent's attempts to self-medicate the depression with alcohol. This compounds the problem because depression is a major side effect of alcohol use.

Causes of Depression. The causes for the onset of depression in young people are many, and no single rule of thumb can be employed to explain all cases.

Some types of depression appear to run in families in generation after generation, and genetics may be contributing to the illness in these cases. A common cause in young people is some form of loss. Losses could include disruptions in attachments to family, peers, or special girlfriends/boyfriends. Disruptions arising from dysfunctional family matters, such as domestic violence or family alcoholism, often result in depression. Disruptions in mastery may also lead to depressed states, especially in the realm of academic failure.

The Nature of Suicide

Suicide is the taking of one's life by one's own hand. The pain of life seems so great that the young person sees death as the only method to relieve this intense suffering. Depressed youth sometimes feel suicidal.

There are two groupings of suicides. The first are true acts of suicide in which the young person clearly wanted to die. The young person thought about it, developed a plan, and then implemented the course of action. The second category is called the suicidal gesture. Here the youngster does not really want to die, but attempts to take his or her life to get attention and help in solving a problem.

For example, John breaks up with his high school sweetheart, Jane. Jane is afraid to lose John, and will also feel embarrassed to be in school, if they are not together. She makes a suicidal gesture by swallowing a bottle of aspirin. She then calls John to tell him what she has done and how she cannot live without him. John becomes understandably frightened, says he will never leave her, and calls an ambulance to take Jane to the hospital where the aspirin are washed out of her system in time. Suicidal gestures are poor ways of resolving conflicts because in the long run they do not work. At some point, John will leave. Gestures are also poor solutions because they are often fatal. Help does not always arrive in time, and many young people do die accidentally.

From 1960 to 1980, the suicide rate for young people between the ages of fifteen and twenty-four years rose from 5.2 per 100,000 to 12.3 per 100,000, a 136 percent increase (Woodarski and Harris, 1996). There has been no appreciable decline similar to this increase in recent years.

Causes of Suicide. As with depressed states, there are again many causes for suicide. In some cases, suicide may be a biological illness. Evidence from Scandinavia on completed suicides (Justice, 1985) found serotonin depletion in the brains of the deceased. Since serotonin is the chemical neurotransmitter that makes us feel good, this finding suggests that some people may be born without the necessary serotonin in their bodies, or that it is metabolized incorrectly in some people. Further research on these findings is currently under way.

Some suicides in today's age may be occurring for the reasons that Durkheim noted. For some young people in an anomic age such as ours, the lack of integration into some aspect of the social fabric may lead to anomic suicides.

Major loss is another common factor in youth suicide. Losses that may precipitate suicide in some young people include school failure, loss of special friends, job failure, sexual issues, problems with drugs, involvement with police, and fear of family censure or public humiliation (Rothman, 1997).

Depression, Suicide, and Violence

Depression may lead to violence against others. The young person is angry with the adult world or with peers over the perceived loss as being unjust. If the loss of self-esteem is seen as too great, taking control of the situation through violence may be seen as the only way to gain the respect of others again. Sometimes the violence involves homicide. More frequently in young people it involves aggravated assault. Depressed young people with a history of violence, a history of substance abuse, and possession of the means for violence are at high risk.

Suicide, often present in depressed states, leads to violence against the self in the form of homicides by guns, knives, ingestion of poisons, and intentional motor vehicle accidents. Young people with a detailed plan, the available means, and problems with substance abuse again are at high risk.

The extent of depression and suicidal thoughts among our children and youth and the severity of violence associated with depression points to the importance of recognizing this first serious warning sign.

Substance Abuse

The Nature of Substance Abuse

Young people often use drugs, including alcohol, to alter their sense of perception and their feeling states, and frequently to alter their bodily states as well. Abuse refers to the use of a drug to the point where it gets the individual into trouble. The trouble may be at home, in school, with peers, with police, in the neighborhood, or with the young person's health as well. Difficulties in any of these areas are all signs of an abuse problem.

If left untreated, the abuse problem may take on the added characteristic of becoming physically addictive. Physiological addiction refers to a biological process in which the drug becomes absorbed into the cells of the youngster's body. This may lead in time to tolerance where the young person loses sensitivity to the psychoactive effects of the drug and requires more of the substance to attain the same high. It may also lead to withdrawal states. Withdrawal states refer to the development of bodily flulike symptoms, when the person stops using the drug and the drug begins to secrete out of the cells of the body.

There are drugs to lift depression, to calm anxiety, to increase excitement, and the like. These drugs can be taken orally, by injection, by inhaling, by insufflation (snorting), transdermally, and rec-

TABLE 2

Drug Abuse: Some Possible Warning Signs:

Bodily States	Poor Motor Coordination, Slurred Speech, Shallow Breathing, Glazed Eyes, Dilated Pupils Decreased Alertness, Drowsiness Loss of Appetite, Disturbed Sleep, Loss of Libido
Feeling States	Depression, Hostility, Irritability, Elation
Behaviors	Appears Intoxicated, Dark Glasses, Drug Paraphernalia, Long-Sleeve Shirt or Blouse

tally. While they may produce the desired change in mental state, they may also be placing the young person at increased risk for cardiovascular disease, pulmonary disease, reproductive problems, neurological damage, and various types of cancer, depending on the type of drug being used.

Table 2 presents an outline of some of the common warning signs of possible drug use, including the use of sunglasses indoors or on cloudy days, and the use of long-sleeve clothing in warm weather to hide needle marks. Since children and adolescents may demonstrate some of these signs in the course of normal growth and development, the list of drug warning signs will be of most assistance if these signs are sudden in onset or persist over a period of time. While one in seven adults is abusing alcohol, two in ten children and adolescents also are, and a great many more are using a variety of additional street drugs.

Causes of Substance Abuse. More is known about alcohol abuse, and we will examine these theories first. Since alcohol abuse tends to run in some families, there is some evidence to suggest that in some familial units, alcoholism may have a genetic base. There is also evidence to suggest that some alcohol abuse is due to hypoglycemic conditions, where the individual is consuming the alcohol for its sugar content. Similarly, some persons with grain allergies to rye, barley, and the like may be consuming the alcohol to address a grain food allergy. Depression and intense anxiety over life stress may also cause some people to begin to abuse alcohol. Finally, there is accumulating medical evidence that anyone may come to abuse alcohol, if the person drinks enough for a long period of time. How much one must drink, for how long a period of time, and what the body's mechanisms are for developing an addictive state are presently unknown.

The research on the causes of drug abuse other than alcohol is newer and still in progress. There may be a biological basis for some drug abuse. For example, some opiate addicts report feeling calm and normal after taking opiates. In these cases, it is hypothesized that perhaps some opiate addicts are born without endorphins, chemicals in the brain that make us feel good when they are circulating in the brain, and use opiates to offset the brain deficiency.

Drug abusers also self-medicate various dysphoric feeling states related to the current pressure from the evolving postindustrial state in which we now find ourselves. Psychiatrist Edward Khantzian (1997) has proposed a way of understanding this process of self-medication. He believes that drug abusers use certain types of drugs for certain types of unpleasant feeling states. In his clinical experience, alcohol and barbiturates are used to reduce anxiety, crack/ cocaine and amphetamines to relieve depression, and opiates to self-medicate states of rage.

Substance Abuse and Violence

Statistics on substance abuse, including alcohol abuse, are difficult to obtain because so much of it is underreported, and, thus, its links to violence are equally difficult to assess. However, even if underreported, the estimates are sobering enough. It is estimated that 50 percent of homicides and assaults and 80 percent of all suicides involve alcohol. Similarly, high rates of alcohol and other drugs have been reported for domestic violence (Strauss and Gelles, 1992). In many cases, young assailants have been just as intoxicated as adults.

Motor vehicle deaths by drunken drivers is another area of substance abuse-related violence. In 1980, there were 1,289,443 arrests for driving under the influence of alcohol (Woodarski, 1989). Of these, 29,957 drivers were under age eighteen, and 696 of these drivers were under age fifteen.

Substance abuse is related to violence primarily because these agents disinhibit the cortical control centers of the brain that inhibit violence and interfere with reasoning, values, and judgment. The side effect of these drugs and the withdrawal process in some substance abusers only compounds the problem and enhances the risk for violent outbursts.

Attention to this second serious warning sign is important in a society saturated with drug use and abuse.

Posttraumatic Stress Disorder

The Nature of Psychological Trauma and PTSD

Psychological trauma refers to the impact of an extreme critical incident on an individual's psychological and physiological functioning (Flannery, 1994a). Trauma may arise when a person is confronted with actual or threatened death or some other threat to one's physical integrity or by witnessing these events happening to others (American Psychiatric Association, 1994). In addition, victims experience intense fear, horror, or helplessness. In children, this intense fear may manifest itself in disorganized or agitated behavior. Common examples of traumatic events include natural and man-made disasters, homicides, hostage-taking, physical and sexual assaults, robberies, major car accidents, and serious life-threatening illnesses.

Children and adults who are traumatized will develop certain symptoms associated with trauma and PTSD. These symptoms may include intrusive recollections of the event, avoidance of the traumatic situation with a loss of general interest in daily activities, and increased physiological arousal. Some of the more common symptoms are listed in table 3, and a complete listing may be found in the American Psychiatric Association's *Diagnostic Manual* (1994).

Intrusive symptoms involve the reexperiencing of the event in images, thoughts, day dreams, and nightmares. Some victims may act

TABLE 3

Some Common Symptoms of Psychological Trauma and PTSD:

Intrusive Symptoms:	Continuous Reexperiencing of the Event in Images, Thoughts, Day Dreams, and Nightmares Acting and Feeling as if Reliving the Event Distress in the Presence of Symbolic Reminders
Avoidant Symptoms:	Avoiding Places and Thoughts Symbolic of the Trauma Problems in Remembering the Event Loss of Interest in Important Activities Restricted Feelings Sense of Foreshortened Future
Psychological Arousal Symptoms:	Hypervigilance Exaggerated Startle Response Sleep Disturbance Difficulty in Concentrating Irritability or Angry Outbursts

or feel as if they were reliving these events, and others may experience great distress in the face of events that remind the victim of the trauma. *Avoidance symptoms* involve avoiding places and thoughts associated with the trauma, problems in remembering the event, a marked loss of interest in other important aspects of the person's life, restricted feelings, and the sense of a foreshortened future. *Physiological arousal symptoms* include difficulties with sleep, hypervigilance, exaggerated startle response, difficulty concentrating, and irritability or angry outbursts in some.

These three symptom clusters may be found in two medical conditions related to traumatic events: Acute Stress Disorder, and in acute, chronic, and delayed onset PTSD. Acute Stress Disorder arises when victims develop these symptoms and some additional symptoms that include, among others, a subjective sense of numbing or detachment, a reduction in awareness of surroundings, or amnesia for the event. Acute Stress Disorder symptoms need to appear within one month of the traumatic incident, and must be present for a minimum of forty-eight hours but no more than four weeks. After one month, the presence of any of the first three symptom clusters (table 3) suggests the presence of PTSD. The diagnosis of acute PTSD is made if these symptoms last for less than three months. Chronic PTSD is determined by the presence of these symptoms for three or more months' duration, and delayed onset PTSD refers to the development of the symptoms for the first time at least six months after the traumatic event.

These severe traumatic crises may also disrupt the victim's sense of reasonable mastery, caring attachments to others, and purposeful meaning in life. These are the very components that become disrupted in the formation of the early warning signs, and these disrupted components are also reflected in the symptoms noted in table 3.

The Psychology of Trauma

By definition, victims experience disruptions in mastery. The nature of the event, frequently interpersonal as in physical abuse, is beyond the person's control, and the victim will remain traumatized until some semblance of control is reinstated. Attachments are also disrupted in at least two ways. First, violence at the hands of another makes the victim realize in a fundamental way that the world is not necessarily safe and that humans cannot necessarily be trusted. To this distrust of others, betrayal may need to be added, if the assailant was someone entrusted with the care of the victim. Many victims understandably withdraw. This withdrawal from others may be compounded by nonvictims who are understandably frightened by what has happened, and come to realize as the victim has just how tenuous the links to Mother Earth are for any of us. Frequently nonvictims end up blaming the victim as a way of providing themselves with the illusion of control. The nonvictims think to themselves that they would not be so careless as the victim was, and thus violence would not happen to them. Dismissed is the fact that violence is random, and can happen to anyone of us at any time. Finally, purposeful meaning is shattered. In the aftermath of an act of violence, the world does not seem orderly, predictable, safe, and worthy of investing energy in it.

There are two additional aspects of psychological trauma that we want to note in passing because they affect many young victims. The first is the overwhelming potential for victims to self-medicate this distress with alcohol and drugs. Unlike other medical problems like cancer, heart disease, or diabetes, many victims of all types of traumatic events go on to develop a substance abuse problem after the traumatic event, and this substance abuse may lead to violence.

The second aspect of trauma refers to the repetition compulsion. One would think that after being a victim of violence one would avoid further violence as best as anyone can. However, that is not the experience of many victims. They return to the scene of the actual crime or some highly similar situation and put themselves in harm's way again. Michelle in the earlier chapter is an example of this. She was sexually abused and then became involved in prostitution for a reason within her that she could not understand. Why do victims like Michelle return to the scene of the crime and repeat what has happened to them? The answer is not fully understood at present, but at least in part it is an attempt by the victim to gain mastery over the situation, to rehearse what has happened, and to learn how one might better protect one's self, should violence ever be encountered again.

The Biology of Trauma

To understand fully the human suffering involved in the lives of young victims and to have a better awareness of how PTSD is related to some acts of violence, a review of the impact of violence on the biology of the victim may be of assistance.

We saw in chapter 2 how an individual's body physiology is mobilized in times of crisis. Adrenaline is converted to epinephrine, and mobilizes the emergency response systems of the body. Heart rate and respiration are strengthened, pupils are dilated for better vision, and sugar is released for greater energy. At the same time, adrenaline is converted to norepinephrine in the brain. Norepinephrine rivets the brain's attention to the crisis at hand in an attempt to save life and avoid injury.

A third chemical grouping that needs to be considered are the endorphins that were mentioned in passing earlier in this chapter. These chemicals lie dormant in the brain. When they begin to circulate in noncrisis situations, the individual feels relaxed and calm. However, when they circulate in moments of traumatic crisis, the endorphins appear to act as analgesics. They deaden pain from any injuries that occur so that the brain's attention to survival is not distracted during the crisis itself. When the immediate crisis has passed, the analgesic effect of the endorphins wears off, and victims will begin to experience pain and suffering, if that has occurred. The endorphins and norepinephrine together appear to produce the best brain chemistry to remember the traumatic event so that victims can learn and remember what is best to do should the victim encounter subsequent traumatic events.

The biology of trauma has one additional painful outcome for many victims, young and old. It is known as *kindling*, and refers to a phenomenon in which small amounts of norepinephrine may produce an emergency response as intense as the original event to some other relatively minor event. It is like a bad case of "frayed nerves." These post-trauma arousal states seem to result from permanent changes in the limbic system due to the continuous presence of norepinephrine in the brain during the original crisis. Kindling is painful because its easily induced state of intense arousal may be produced by the small increments in norepinephrine associated with both pleasant and unpleasant events. For example, a traumatized youngster with a kindled brain may experience intrusive memories of being hit by his stepfather, when he hears an argument by strangers in another room. Sadly, this same youngster may also have intrusive memories of these assaults when riding his bicycle or swimming in a pool. In part, this is why youth victims of violence withdraw and avoid not only reminders of the traumatic event, but also life activities that are inherently pleasant.

Psychological Trauma, PTSD, and Violence

Trauma and possible subsequent violence are potentially linked in several ways. First, children who have been victims of violence may have deficiencies in intellectual, emotional, and social functioning. These deficiencies limit problem-solving skills, and increase the possibility of violent solutions. Second, as we have seen, many trauma victims self-medicate their untreated PTSD with drugs or alcohol, and thereby increase the risk of disinhibiting the cortical control centers of their own brains. Third, many victims of violence become depressed and attempt suicide. Fourth, the kindling phenomenon in the brains of some victims may lead to aggressive outbursts in some instances. Lastly, children who are direct victims or victim witnesses may learn that violence works and is an acceptable solution in solving conflicts. A recent study of adult prisoners who were victims of violence earlier in their lives (Collins and Baily, 1990) found that, for those with at least one PTSD symptom and an arrest history for previous violence, the PTSD symptom preceded or occurred in the same year as the arrest for violence. This suggests that PTSD symptoms in adults may have a causal role in the onset of violence, a finding similar to that of Dr. Widom (1989) for young people.

As in the case of depression and substance abuse, the links to subsequent violence in this third serious warning sign, PTSD, are clear. The toll in human suffering and the risk for subsequent violence illustrate the pain associated with both aspects of violence. In the absence of treatment, neither aggressor nor victim is ever free.

This completes our review of the three serious warning signs. It is clear that not responding to the early warning signs has important implications. For the youngster with disruptions in mastery, attachments, and meaning, the chances of developing the more serious consequences of depression, substance abuse, and untreated PTSD increase appreciably. These serious warning signs cause more intense suffering, and require more time to be treated successfully. They also place all young people, as well as the adult community, at risk for more severe and more frequent violence from those youngsters with the serious warning signs, serious violence that might not have happened had the warning signs been identified and the youngster's problem corrected.

If the adult care giving community disregards both the early and serious warning signs, then it is almost certain that violence will follow because the third warning signs have to do with conduct disorder. This is the most urgent of the warning signs. Here, youths are already engaging in a variety of violent acts and are well on their way to a life of adult antisocial and criminal behavior. Conduct disordered children place all of us in harm's way, and this disorder is the sole focus of the next chapter.

5

URGENT WARNING SIGNS:
CONDUCT DISORDER

Loneliness and the feeling of being unwanted
Is the most terrible poverty.
—Mother Teresa

And where is now my hope?
—Job 17:15

"Sergent McKenzie, Smithvale Police Department, this call is being recorded."

"This is Lenny Marchant. I just found my brother Tony in the closet. He don't look so good." . . .

"How do you plead to the charge of armed robbery, young man?"

"Guilty, Your Honor."

"I remand you to the Department of Youth Services for a period not to exceed two years."

Judge Richard Winslow, who had been the presiding judge in the Smithvale juvenile court for twenty-two years, sat back from the bench. Seen one delinquent, he thought, seen them all. Why did they do such things?

Lenny had been before Judge Winslow eleven times on a variety of charges, including cruelty to animals, car theft, selling drugs, grand larceny, and now armed robbery. How did kids end up like this? Was it the parents? The schools? What? . . .

No doubt the answers to these questions involve complicated matters, but it is a safe guess that in Lenny's case that October day in the fourth grade when he came home from school contributed to today's judicial proceedings. For it was on that day that his permanent distrust of the world began.

Lenny came home to the empty house, poured himself a glass of milk, and then went looking for his baseball mitt. When he checked behind the closet door, he found his younger brother, Tony, on the floor. Tony's skull had been bashed to a pulp, his blood had since congealed, and his skin was cold to the touch.

Lenny was more afraid than he had ever been in his short life, and phoned his mother at work. His father was a letter carrier, his mother did piecework in a factory that made printed circuit boards for computers, and both were frequently in an alcoholic haze. His mother said that she was too busy to leave work and that Lenny should call the police for help. As Lenny feared, when the police later told his parents that Tony was dead, neither parent seemed distressed.

For a year and a half, there had been some relief. Lenny was placed in a foster home where he ate regularly, was required to do his homework, and slept through the night without parental fights. He even had a long overdue dental appointment.

This came to an end, however, when he was returned to the custody of his parents, an event that occurred when Lenny's Uncle Joey was charged with Tony's murder. Apparently, the murder was precipitated by Tony's plans to tell his teacher that Uncle Joey was sodomizing him.

Kill or be killed. Survival first. Trust no one.

John Donne was not fully correct. Sometimes, a child is forced to become an island because there appears to be no other workable solution.

The subject matter of this chapter is the last of the warning signs on the continuum: the urgent warning signs. These urgent warning signs are the most grave because the child is already committing frequent acts of violence that are placing everyone at risk, and, if ignored, will only worsen over the course of the child's life. The urgent warning signs are associated with conduct disorder, and culminate when the early and serious warning signs are left unaddressed.

This outgrowth can be clearly seen in Lenny's short life. First, he experienced disruptions in mastery, attachments, and meaning. Parental alcoholism and parental physical abuse made his home life both stressful and unpleasant. His attachments to his parents and brother appear distant. From his court record we know that he was deficient in interpersonal and academic skills, and that same court record suggests an apparent disregard for others.

These unattended early warning signs led to depression and PTSD. When these too were ignored, the urgent warning signs associated with conduct disorder took root, a disorder fraught with violence toward person and property, and a cavalier disregard for society's norms. If left unattended, the urgent warning signs of conduct disorder place the young person at high risk for an adult life of violence and crime. While youth violence can also arise from inattention to the early and serious warning signs, the frequency and severity of untreated conduct disorder has the more persistent negative consequences over time.

In this chapter we examine three issues highly interrelated with youth violence: adult antisocial personality disorder, childhood conduct disorder, and the indicators of impending loss of control.

Antisocial Personality Disorder

Antisocial persons are those adult individuals who are violent, criminal, and without a sense of moral responsibility. Some of the main characteristics of antisocial persons are noted in table 1.

The antisocial person is characterized by violence toward persons and property, including the major crimes of homicide, rape, robbery, and assault as well as destruction of property. No one is safe, and anyone and anything may become a focus of this destructiveness. Deceitfulness is a second common characteristic. Pathological lying, conning others for pleasure or profit, and failure to honor basic social obligations at home, at work, or in the community are common. The deceitfulness may be socially charming or rude and coarse. A third common factor in antisocial persons is a fundamental and persistent failure to conform to society's basic norms. These individuals frequently act on impulse, have no concern for the safety of others, and experience no apparent sense of guilt or remorse. Substance abuse with impaired reasoning and disinhibition of the cor-

TABLE 1

Signs of Antisocial Personality Disorder:

1. *Violence toward Person and Property*
   Homicide, Rape, Robbery, Assault
   Destruction of Property

2. *Deceitfulness*
   Pathological Lying
   Conning Others for Pleasure or Profit
   Failure to Honor Social Responsibilities

3. *Failure to Conform to Social Norms*
   Disregard for Safety of Others
   Impulsive
   No Remorse, Moral Depravity

4. *Age of Onset*   Over Age 18 with Conduct disorder Before Age 15

tical control centers of the brain compound an already very serious situation.

Chapter 2 catalogued the many causes of violence, and antisocial persons have several of them. While these persons often have abnormal electroencephalograph readings, a high frequency of ADHD, and untreated PTSD, these biological factors alone do not explain these lives of crime, since many citizens have these biological issues, and do not become violent. More relevant may be the social and psychological causes associated with the anomic cycle of violence.

In an earlier book (Flannery, 1997), I reviewed ten studies of young and adult offenders that numbered 10,800 persons. The offenders were from both genders, all races, creeds, and ethnic groups, and all geographical areas of the country. The studies spanned a fifty-year period, and the findings were remarkably consistent. These offenders came from homes with disrupted attachments to family units that included divorce, desertion, separation, foster home placement, and parental incarceration. Similarly, there were disrupted attachments due to dysfunctional family life, including domestic violence, parental alcoholism, gambling, erratic discipline, and profound social isolation. Inadequate mastery was common in the form of interpersonal skill deficiencies and academic failure, situations that resulted in anger and feelings of inferiority. Disruptions in meaning were widespread and resulted in the failure to conform to social norms, as we have noted.

Males have a lifetime risk of antisocial personality disorder of 4.5-5.0 percent. For females, the lifetime risk is currently estimated at 0.8-1.0 percent. In both genders, antisocial personality disorder declines substantially by age forty-five.

Conduct Disorder

If antisocial personality disorder is one serious outcome of youth violence left unattended, conduct disorder is one of its more fertile training grounds. Table 2 captures some of conduct disorder's more common features that make these warning signs urgent in nature.

In these youngsters, violence toward person and property has already begun to occur. While homicide is less frequent, assault, robbery, and forced sexual activity are not. Conduct disordered youngsters commit acts of cruelty to people and animals, as well as acts of vandalism, including fire setting. They lie to blame others to escape the consequences of their own actions or to manipulate others for their own ends. They do not internalize society's values, and are often impulsive as evidenced by acts of truancy and running away. They show no guilt or remorse, and many are morally depraved.

These youngsters frequently have co-occurring problems with ADHD and PTSD. They are academic underachievers, respond poorly to discipline, and engage in smoking, drinking, and sexual activity at early ages. They attempt to fend off their sense of poor self-esteem by means of crime and violence. In doing so, they are often motivated by monetary rewards, by the thrill of the chase, and by the chance to increase their power and dominance among their delinquent peers. They also have a higher suicide rate.

Writer Gail Stewart (1997) has recorded the lives of some of these troubled youngsters to help parents, teachers, and adult care givers

TABLE 2

Urgent Warning Signs of Conduct Disorder:

---

1. *Violence toward Person and Property*
   Assault, Robbery, Forced Sexual Activity
   Cruelty to People or Animals
   Vandalism, Fire Setting

2. *Deceitfulness*
   Lying

3. *Failure to Conform to Social Norms*
   Truant or Run Away
   Impulsive
   No Remorse, Moral Depravity

4. *Age of Onset*   Under Age 18

---

to develop a greater understanding of the developmental havoc in these children that leads to the urgent warning signs and episodes of violence.

In one example, she reports on a young male teenager who as a young child was beaten with belts, extension cords, and broomsticks, and was thrown down stairs by his stepfather. He found his sister dead in her crib with her mouth open and her tongue rolled back. When his mother could not cope with the child's death, he did the family's cooking and cleaning. His later adolescence led to arson, drugs, and prison.

This youngster's life was similar in many ways to the life of Lenny Marchant described earlier in this chapter. Both witnessed traumatic events, both had inadequate parental support, both had to take on parental responsibilities far beyond their years, and both they and their subsequent victims paid a heavy toll in human suffering. Both of these young lives graphically illustrate that violence breeds violence.

In assessing the urgent warning signs, youth care givers should look for patterns of this disorder, and not episodic instances (Samenow, 1989). Caution must be used in assessing the presence of these urgent warning signs where antisocial behaviors might be an attempt to respond to a hostile environment. In these latter cases, the motivation of the youngster must be fully evaluated. For example, if a youngster is threatening others with a weapon on the way to school, does this mean the weapon is for protection on the streets in a neighborhood of drug dealers by a child who is otherwise socially compliant? Or is this a pattern of behavior in an angry youngster with poor self-esteem and no sense of remorse?

The incidence of conduct disorder in males under age eighteen is 6-16 percent, and in females under age eighteen, 2-9 percent. Conduct disordered boys are more likely to fight, steal, and vandalize, whereas conduct disordered girls are more prone to lying, truancy, substance abuse, and prostitution.

The need for immediate attention to the urgent warning signs can be seen by comparing the characteristics of antisocial personality disorder in table 1 with those of conduct disorder in table 2. Child specialists Kenneth Magid and Carole McKelvey (1987) drew attention to these similarities over a decade ago, and I have updated the comparison for our anomic age. The comparisons in violent behavior and antisocial values is strikingly similar, with conduct disordered behavior in many ways being a degree of difference in severity rather than kind.

The urgent warning signs are just that: urgent.

Impending Loss of Control

While the goals of adult care providers are to identify the early, serious, and urgent warning signs in children in order to solve the underlying problems before violence erupts, there may be instances in this process before a youngster's needs are fully identified where the youngster may be in tenuous control or lose control altogether. At this point, both other children as well as adults are at risk for imminent harm. In the interest of preventive safety, some indicators of impending loss of control may be found in table 3. The presence of these indicators does not mean that violence will necessarily occur, but their presence suggests a greater risk of possible loss of control. A helpful rule of thumb is this: the greater the number of indicators present, the greater the risk for violence.

TABLE 3

Indicators of Impending Loss of Control:

1. *Known Medical or Psychiatric Condition Associated with Violence*

2. *Appearance*
   Disorganized in Physical Appearance or in Dress
   Tensed Facial Expression
   Glazed Eyes
   Inappropriate Use of Sunglasses
   Long Sleeves in Warm Weather

3. *Behaviors*
   Behavioral Signs of Severe Agitation
   Verbally Argumentative
   Suggestions of Substance Abuse
   Verbal Threats
   Threat of Weapons
   Past History of Violence toward Others

There are three areas of concern. The first is the awareness of any of known medical or psychiatric condition that may result in violence. While these are not common causes of violence, their presence in any given young person should be considered a risk factor.

The second area of concern is the appearance of the child or teenager. A youngster whose physical appearance or dress is disorganized and out of the ordinary may be having problems with control. Similarly, tensed facial expressions or fists may indicate attempts to hold anger in. Glazed eyes, sunglasses on cloudy days or indoors, and long-sleeve clothing on warm days may all be signs of substance abuse with possible cortical dyscontrol.

The final area is the actual behavior of the young person. Signs of severe agitation (e.g., brisk walking back and forth, pacing, pounding on objects), verbal argumentativeness and verbal threats are also signs of impending or actual loss of control. Suggestions of substance abuse (e.g., smell of alcohol, walks unevenly), and a past history of violence toward others are additional indicators. The threat of the use of weapons toward the self or others should **always** be taken seriously. It is better to be conservative in these cases and be wrong than to be less cautious and find several children dead at school or in the neighborhood.

This concludes our review of the continuum of increasingly severe warning signs. Each of the groupings of early, serious, and urgent warning signs has been correlated with subsequent instances of youth violence in some children. While some of the early warning signs may seem innocuous at first (e.g., divorce), if left unattended, they may develop over time into the serious and urgent warning signs with their increased probabilities for serious violence. Even if violence were never to erupt, our children should not have to endure the suffering associated with any of the warning signs.

In this light, the final chapter considers what can be done to prevent youth violence once the warning signs have been recognized. The adult care giver community has a variety of strategies from which to choose, and these are presented in part 3.

PART THREE

YOUTH VIOLENCE: SOLUTIONS AND RESOURCES

Dateline: San Francisco. May 12, 1995.

For twenty minutes? Dear God, no. Was she in pain? Did she slip into unconsciousness toward the end? Such were the thoughts of her parents as they reviewed the final twenty minutes of her life yet again. Far away, bulldozers moved efficiently in clouds of dust to remove the last traces of the church and its tragedy.

Adolescence can be a troubling time and so it was for one young woman. Many teens hope that a change of scenery will help sort things out. This young woman was one of them, and so she ran away from the woods of Oregon to the streets of San Francisco. I might as well have a new beginning, she thought, and renamed herself with her favorite uncle's nickname.

Life on the streets and in homeless shelters was not quite as glamorous as it seemed, when escape from pressure was the goal. The young girl became understandably depressed, and, apparently, had passing thoughts of suicide.

In the darkness of the night, the runaway met a sixteen-year-old girl and her twenty-three-year-old male companion. They took the runaway to a burned-out Baptist church on Delores Street, where several squatters passed their days. They introduced her to their Druid-like religion, and painted her face with red stars and moons and crosses.

Then, at 4:30 A.M., they killed her. Slowly. Deliberately. In cold blood. One held the cord around her neck. The other held her down. Slowly. Methodically. For the next twenty minutes, they gradually asphyxiated her. She gasped for breath. She struggled to be freed. She turned blue. Firmly. Deliberately. Her killers held her still until every last ounce of breath had been wrenched from her body.

And when they were done, they stuffed the runaway's body in the church's ladder well, and went downstairs to sleep.

Delores Street: From the Spanish for sorrows.

Sorrows that will be permanently etched into the minds and hearts of the young girl's parents until their deaths.

This third and final section of the book examines the resources and strategies that are available for preventing youth violence. Again, there are several possible questions to consider:

1. Can anything really be done to prevent youth violence?
2. What is the best method for identifying the various warning signs?
3. What are the best strategies for determining the needs underlying these warning signs?
4. What are helpful intervention strategies?
5. Can these strategies be linked to addressing the larger issue of the anomic cycle of violence?

6

PREVENTING
YOUTH VIOLENCE

And in today, already walks tomorrow.
—Samuel Taylor Coolidge

Love bears all things.
—I Corinthians 13:7

He stopped the car, thought for a moment, and then got out. He felt uneasy, but he walked over anyway.

"Hi, mother. I told you that I'd be back to visit. It's been a while, and, even though it is still difficult for me, I am here to be with you.

"I want to begin by apologizing for that period in my life when I caused you so much sorrow. I regret that we argued so much, that I stole money from your purse, and that I got drunk more times than I can count. I know now that it was a difficult time for me, but I am still saddened at the pain that I caused everyone in the family. Since words don't come easily to me, I have written a short poem to express my thanks to you. Let me read it now.

> *I was consumed with rage,*
> *and you calmed me.*
> *I felt like damaged goods,*
> *and you valued me.*
> *I wanted to destroy myself,*
> *and you protected me.*
> *I was filled with self-hate,*
> *and you loved me.*
> *Thank you for being there."*

With that, on this cold February morning, the seventh anniversary of her death, her foster son knelt down gently, and placed his poem and a single red rose on the grave site of the woman who had taken him in and saved his life from a violent end.

Even after seven years, the snow associated with her death still fell heavy on his heart.

As this vignette suggests, troubled youth can be helped before violence has run its course. There are remedies and interventions that are helpful. However, this example also demonstrates that addressing these matters does not necessarily run smoothly, and that perseverance on the part of the child and the parent, teacher, or counselor is necessary.

Preventing youth violence by addressing the needs of individuals is best understood as part of a more comprehensive approach to youth violence that includes prevention at home and in the community (Flannery, 1997) and in work sites (Flannery, 1995). Interested adults, especially professional counselors, may wish to supplement the efforts for individual youths with these larger programmatic prevention efforts for groups of children as a whole.

This chapter outlines the process for assessing the presence of the warning signs of youth violence and for implementing the five basic guidelines for intervention. These should be considered as starting points, and are not meant to make each reader a professional counselor nor to serve as a text for child rearing. The five guidelines present some helpful suggestions based on the experiences of many parents, teachers, and counselors in successfully addressing the issues underlying the presence of the warning signs in children and adolescents. In the last analysis, however, they are guidelines, and some part of a guideline may not be helpful with some aspect of a specific child's need. In these cases, that aspect of the guideline may need to be rejected or modified. Ultimately, it is the individual parent or care giver who is responsible for the child, and the parent or care giver's judgment in specific instances should take precedence.

Appendix A provides additional potential resources for adults in the form of national associations and societies that focus on preventing youth violence from a wide range of perspectives.

TABLE 1

The Continuum of Warning Signs:

Early Warning Signs	Biological Markers
	Disrupted Attachments: Disruptions in Family Unit, Dysfunctional Family Unit, Absence of Peer Group, Disrupted Relationships at School or in Neighborhood
	Disruptions in Reasonable Mastery: Deficiencies in Personal Growth, Interpersonal Growth, Academics
	Disruptions in Meaning: Disavows Prosocial Values, Disregard for Others
Serious Warning Signs	Depression (with Suicidal Thinking)
	Substance Abuse
	Posttraumatic Stress Disorder
Urgent Warning Signs	Conduct Disorder

Guidelines for Assessing and Resolving the Warning Signs

Assessment

The General Process

Table 1 presents a summary of the early, serious, and urgent warning signs. The key to the assessment procedure is to identify potential warning signs, to note the level of severity of the warning signs, and to infer what the normal development process is that has gone awry and that needs to be corrected.

For example, children of divorce have disrupted attachments in the basic family unit. Children of alcoholics also have disrupted attachments because of dysfunctional family units. Suicidal children are depressed, and may have untreated PTSD and substance abuse. Children who disregard the worth of others have not had an attachment figure to teach them more prosocial values. In general, the clearer our understanding of what is causing the warning signs, the easier it will be for us to identify the needed resources to remedy the problem.

The assessment of the child's needs can be conducted in a variety of ways. The child's self-report of how he or she feels can be a first step. However, since children are sometimes inaccurate in their self-evaluations, other pieces of information may be needed to confirm the child's actual state. These indicators may come from knowing the youngster's personal life history, from observations by others and oneself, and from behavioral indicators that might include interpersonal skills, poor grades, and the formal warning signs that have been noted. In some cases, there may be information from medical and psychological tests. These pieces of information are especially important, if the observations are of sudden changes such as in grades, peer group, or boyfriend/girlfriend relationships. Sudden changes may indicate a recent event that has left the child overwhelmed.

When this information has raised the concern of the adult, the next step is to raise the issue tactfully. Families differ in their sense of values and sense of privacy, and schools and counselors themselves also have a number of different cultures and policies. Basic questions need to be considered by the parent, teacher, counselor, or other care giver. Whom can I trust with my concerns? Who would be an objective person to evaluate my observations? If my observations are correct, who would be the best person to begin to help me gather resources to address the child's need(s)? Who would be the best person to approach the child in time? The parent? The teacher? The pediatrician? A clergy person? Care should be taken not to place the child in the middle of competing authorities and not to let the child play one adult off against the other.

If the presence of the warning signs is confirmed, then the adults involved need to infer as best they can the probable developmental cause for the warning sign, and to begin to reflect on what resources will be needed to help the youngster. If several adults are involved (e.g., parent, teacher, and school guidance counselor for a child in a poor peer-group situation), one person needs to be identified as the person who will be the primary individual to form a secure attachment with the child in addressing this issue.

Various strategies and resources for assistance need to be considered. Since child rearing, as noted, is a complex matter, most strategies to address the underlying issues behind the warning signs will involve several components. Chapter 2 outlines the various factors associated with youth violence, and chapter 3 summarizes the basic components of the normal developmental processes of mastery, attachments, and meaning. The information in these chapters can serve as suggestions for what may be needed to correct the problems. These resources need to be prioritized and adapted to the specific circumstances of the child. For example, the adults may agree on the need to provide access to a peer group. If a child is interested in athletics, a sports peer group might be a solution. However, if the child is interested in music, joining the school band might be a better answer.

It might be wise to consider appointing a "case manager" to oversee all the components of the child's needed resources. In health care, a case manager may or may not provide a treatment intervention, but is there to act as the patient's advocate, to see that all needed treatments are provided, and to be sure that the care givers regularly communicate with one another. Similarly, for young people at risk, one of the adults could assume the role of case manager. It may or may not be the parent or primary attachment person. In any event, the case manager assumes the administrative responsibility for seeing that the problem is corrected.

When the warning sign is confirmed, its underlying cause has been clarified, the needed resources have been gathered, and the case manager and the parent or primary person are in place, the team then needs to begin to address the warning sign in small, manageable steps so that neither the child nor the treatment team is overwhelmed and so that both parties may experience some initial success in mastery. Obvious exceptions to this general rule of approach include any crisis situations, such as a child brandishing a weapon or a child in medical or psychiatric crisis. These matters need to be attended to immediately.

General Rules

Three general rules are helpful in guiding the assessment process. The first is: the sooner, the better. Obviously, recognizing the warning signs early on lessens the suffering of the child, and hastens the return to more normal development. Many children suffer needlessly because adults dismiss the warning signs, and assume the child is in a phase and will grow out of it. Warning signs can be identified and remedied long before the child reaches the stage of violence. In a similar fashion, early warning signs should not be considered relatively benign. All warning signs have the potential for serious subsequent violent outbursts.

A second general rule is that multiple warning signs may suggest a greater risk for violence. The more signs there are, and the more severe that they are on the continuum of severity, the more likely it is that the child may be overwhelmed and may act impulsively in frustration and anger.

Finally, some warning signs and youth issues will warrant professional care. A parent may be able to help a child cope with a divorce, but it would not be reasonable to expect that parent to deal solely with an adolescent that was suicidally depressed. Not every parent, teacher, or counselor is expected to excel in all matters, and professional resources should be considered when they are needed.

Intervention

General Considerations

Below are five basic guidelines to assist counselors, teachers, and parents who are attempting to take steps to prevent youth violence. These guidelines are those that have been found to be the most helpful for the greatest number of children and teenagers. They are arranged in general order of importance, and the individual(s) who is providing assistance may find that several guidelines may need to be utilized at once. With the exception of the first step, safety, the parent or care giver should assume flexibility among these gidelines, and design the needed intervention to the specific needs of the child.

These guidelines are based on restoring, reinstituting, or creating for the first time the normal components of growth and development in the child where they have been disrupted. They also address the various aspects of the anomic cycle of violence that we have spoken of, the cycle with its disrupted social fabric in an era that emphasizes material goods and may lead to depression, anger, substance abuse, and violence in many of our youth. These five guidelines listed below have been designed to address societal needs in this general anomic social climate as well as the needs of specific individual children.

Child development is complicated, and these steps will take time to be successfully implemented. Expect resistance. The various warning signs in table 1 are the result of the child's trust being disrupted in some fundamental way. From the child's perspective, there is no reason to be eager to trust the adult world again and to face possible further harm or rejection. However, with patience, the team as a whole will succeed over time, since most warning signs are reversible. This is especially true for the early warning signs. The biological markers that may cause some of these disruptions are addressed in the fourth guideline.

The Basic Guidelines

1. Safety First

Preventing actual, immediate violence is the first step to ensure the safety of other children and adults, and the safety of the youth assailant. There are a range of possible unsafe situations. Some of the more common issues and suggestions for possible intervention are briefly outlined here. It is the primary responsibility of the adults confronting these safety matters to do what they feel is best, and their best judgment in a specific instance should always come first.

Actual Use of Weapon. If the child is out of control and is using a weapon or threatening to use one, seek the physical safety of everyone first. Put other children and adults in the immediate area under cover. Alert possible innocent bystanders, and call the police. Rushing the child or trying to talk the child down are actions fraught with danger, but are sometimes considered in the most extreme and extenuating circumstances. Little is gained if the adult is killed or seriously wounded, and the rampage continues.

Coma or Serious Medical Injury. In the aftermath of youth violence, some children may need emergency medical attention. This may also occur in acts of attempted suicide that include slashing, gun shots, or overdosing on prescription medicines or street drugs. Call for emergency medical services. In the interim, staunch any profuse bleeding, and perform cardiopulmonary resuscitation (CPR) and first aid if you have been trained to do so and if they are needed. Gather information on the type of injury or the chemical agent ingested. This information may be gathered from physical evidence at the scene, such as drug paraphernalia, or from other observers, such as members of a peer group. Since many of these situations are crime scenes, try not to touch the possible evidence, but note where it is so that the emergency medical technicians can be apprised of the possible cause of the injury or coma. The police will handle the evidence when they arrive on scene.

Acute Suicidal Thoughts or Plans. If you believe that a child may have suicidal thoughts or plans, the following general questions may be helpful in gathering initial information for medical or counseling personnel. Ask if the child wants to kill him- or herself. If the answer is yes, then get the child to a local hospital emergency room immediately and do not leave the child alone in the interim. If the child answers no to the first question, proceed to the second question. Does the child have a plan? Here, the adult is listening for a well-formulated plan. The child who reports a fully loaded revolver in his school locker has a more thought-out plan than a child who says he will think of something when the time comes. Well-formulated plans should be taken seriously, and immediate assistance should be sought. If the child answers no to the first two questions, a third question is asked: What keeps you alive? Here, the adult wants to assess the support network of the child and the child's reasons to live. A statement such as "my parents really care and I'm on the baseball team" indicate greater support than "only my cat loves me."

Always take any statements of suicidal thoughts or plans seriously, and have them evaluated immediately by professional counselors and other medical personnel. Better to be conservative and wrong and have the child alive than to be less conservative and correct, and have the child dead. If it turns out that the statements were a gesture for attention, the emergency room personnel will help you find counseling assistance. Make your evaluation based on what the child is saying, not on how distressed the child may or may not appear. Some children and adolescents who have decided to kill themselves are relieved to have reached the decision and are very calm in their last hours. Finally, when asking the initial questions, the child's answers may be further compromised and less accurate if the child has been abusing drugs or alcohol.

Assault. If a child is combative and actually out of control, seek safety for yourself and others, and call the police or school security. If the child displays the indicators of impending loss of control, but is still in tenuous control, the adult may want to talk the child down. Stand back seven feet, try to identify the child's perceived grievance, tell the child that you have sent for help, and try to ally yourself with the child's perceived injustice in terms of trying to get that matter addressed. Keep the child talking until help arrives. Then do what you can to see that the child's issue is addressed. Should the child report the presence of a weapon during this process, ask the child to place the weapon in a neutral third corner. Do not reach for it as the child may have a second concealed weapon.

Rape. Children and adults who are victims of rape at the hands of other youth need to do what is needed for survival. Various strategies can be considered, but no strategy works in every case, and the presence of a weapon further complicates what can be done safely. Some victims stall for time, others yell, some run away. Still others vomit, pick their noses, or act crazy. In any case, the victim should try to get a clear description of the assailant for police.

Robbery. If a child or adult is being robbed by a young person, the victim should not resist. Give what is asked and do not try to hold something back. Victims who have turned over their wallets but kept several dollars in another pocket have been shot by youths who perceive this as an insult to their authority. Material goods may be replaced. A victim's life cannot.

The one exception to offering no resistance in robberies occurs in those instances where the person is being taken hostage. In these cases, every reasonable attempt should be made to resist and flee. Again, the presence of a weapon complicates the decisions that need to be made in these cases.

Domestic Violence. Since domestic violence occurs within the privacy of the home, it is harder to detect. If violence is overheard occurring in an apartment or a house, the police should be called. Some state governments also have "800" numbers where citizens can report their concerns anonymously.

Sexual abuse in the absence of overt physical injuries and the symptoms of PTSD is hard to assess. However, there are often observable signs of physical abuse of children. These may include bruises on the facial cheeks or body, unusual marks on the body, burns, a distended stomach, frequent accidents, or unusually aggressive or socially isolated behaviors. Children who are observed to be hitting others have frequently been direct victims of, or witnesses to, physical abuse by others.

School Safety. Crisis prevention through environmental design can be implemented in school systems. Here, the superintendent or principal may want to consider the following. School systems have reported success with metal detectors, police presence, dogs that sniff lockers periodically, penalties for weapons possession, courses on antiviolence strategies, verbal-conflict resolution methods, and adults on alert in the building. In some systems, background investigations of staff and teachers have also been included.

When the safety of all has been addressed in any of these situations, the remaining four guidelines can be considered.

2. Fostering Attachments

The fundamental root cause of all of the warning signs in almost all cases is the failure of some important attachment to be formed or maintained. Thus, parents and other adults who seek to reverse the warning signs will by necessity be involved to some degree in fostering attachments with the identified youngster. Children who have experienced disruptions in attachments feel betrayed and will not easily trust again.

To address this need, it is important for the adult care giver to be a constant presence in the child's life. For trust to be restored, there must be consistent and predictable behavior on the part of the adult care giver as well as prosocial values that are stated and then incorporated in the actions of the adults who seek to be trusted.

With the backdrop for trust in place, the care giver may want to examine the child's capacities and needs for empathy, sharing, grieving, and true self-esteem. The basic components for normal development in each of these areas were outlined in chapter 3, and these components can be adapted to the specific needs of the child. The child may need support and training in many of these areas, since disruptions in attachments usually impact on several of these areas at the same time.

As this process continues, the care giver may also want to consider fostering helpful attachments to the child's peer group. Groups are important to children because they provide attachments outside of the home. Prosocial groups provide acceptance, preclude isolation and feelings of vulnerability, teach mastery skills by learning from others, and instill a sense of purpose.

Teachers may have a special role to play in the formation of attachments outside of the home (Weinstein, 1995). In many ways, teachers are able to function as parental substitutes for those children who may have parenting needs. Teachers have the elements of parental authority in terms of social power, wisdom, competence, and the ability to nurture children emotionally. Teachers are in a unique position to provide nonfamilial protection and support.

3. Fostering Mastery

With safety and the beginning foundations for attachments in place, the parent or primary care giver, case manager, and treatment team will next want to consider how best to restore, instill, or refine the child's mastery skills in the areas of personal growth, interpersonal growth, and academic achievement. The team will want to consider how best to teach the child the skills that he or she needs to master.

One helpful general approach is to teach the child the skills that are associated with resilient children and adults (Bloom, 1996; Flannery, 1994b, Masten and Coatsworth, 1998). These skills are associated with good physical and mental health, and a sense of well-being, and are helpful in mitigating the potential negative effects associated with life's many adversities. Resilient children and adults are rarely violent.

The skills of resilient children are those that have been spoken of throughout the book: at least one, consistent, caring attachment; reasonable mastery skills; a basic healthy lifestyle; a network of friends; and concern for the welfare of others. It is not by accident that these skills form the five basic guidelines for successful intervention in resolving the early warning signs. They are the basis of sound development.

Any needed discipline during this process should be warm, caring, and firm with reasonable expectations, and with both rewards and penalties. This approach may be different from the inconsistent, harsh, or violent discipline that has marked the lives of some children, and these youngsters will need some extra time to learn the new system. They may test the limits of the new system early on to see if the discipline is in fact reasonable, consistent, and fair.

The fundamental goal in fostering mastery is to reverse the warning signs by teaching the child the skills the child will need now and in the future. It is also a good way to develop the child's sense of true self-esteem, one that is based on an accurate perception of one's strengths and weaknesses.

4. Medical and Psychiatric Conditions

At times, biological factors may assume greater importance in some violent outbursts. For example, at one time I was asked to conduct neuropsychological testing on a ninth grade girl. She had had excellent grades through grade eight, but then proceeded to fail grade nine three years in a row. Her angry parents were convinced that she was not studying and stood guard outside her room at night to make sure that she was doing her homework. After the third failed year, the principal ordered her not to return to school until she changed her bad attitude. The youngster alternated between states of anger and sadness, and everyone was very tense. The neuropsychological testing revealed that she had a dysgraphia, an inability to write out what she was thinking. It was suggested to the school that she be given oral exams, which had been the case through grade eight, and she passed with high grades. The anger that might have resulted in violence dissolved.

To avoid missing medical problems such as these, every child should have a full physical exam and a psychological exam that should cover the areas of neuropsychological intactness, intelligence, skills and aptitudes, and personality features. Medical problems can be ruled out, and the gathered information will be of immense value in developing remedial interventions that are fully tailored to a child's individual needs.

The parent or primary care giver and the case manager will also want to consider the child's temperament, and how specific interventions may be further tailored. For example, a sensation-seeking youngster may need many different tasks; an impulsive child may need extra learning trials for mastering frustration tolerance and delay of gratification.

Specific medical interventions may be needed for the serious warning signs of depression, substance abuse, PTSD, and for the urgent warning signs of conduct disorder. Parents, primary care givers and case managers may want to consult the child's physician or professional therapist. The advice of these specialists should always be heeded.

Depression is a medical illness, and there are a variety of ways to treat this warning sign. In cases where the depression is due primarily to loss, grieving the loss (see guideline 5), and finding new direction in life after the loss can be very helpful to the child or adolescent. Talking things out, expressing anger and sadness, and starting out on new adventures can lift the depression in many youths.

In those cases, where the depression may have genetic roots or the loss has been so severe that the youngster has become biologically depressed, medicines and other medical interventions may be of great assistance in restoring the youngster's normal biological functioning and general level of energy. Grieving may be an additional needed component of care in some of these. In cases where the depressed youngster has suicidal thoughts or behaviors, a brief hospitalization in a nearby medical facility may be needed to contain the youngster's self-destructive rage. This may be especially true for a suicidally depressed teenager who is being given antidepressant medication. At some point in the first thirty days of taking the medicine, the teenager's body will become re-energized enough to act on the suicidal thoughts, but not energized enough as yet to feel that the depression has lifted. The brief hospital visit during this period helps to contain the suicidal preoccupations during this interim period until the medicine has begun to treat the depression effectively.

Since substance abuse may disinhibit cortical control, as noted, destroy general health, wreak havoc on family life, and interfere with traumatic memory recall in cases where substances are being used to self-medicate untreated PTSD, it is important that the youngster's plans for growth include a substance abuse treatment component.

In cases of long-standing addictions, a medically supervised detoxification process may need to be included. The detoxification is to remove the bulk of the offending substance from the youngster's body safely and without undue side effects.

In these and other cases where detoxification has not been needed, ongoing counseling and support are necessary until it is clear to the adult care givers that the addictive pattern of behavior has stopped. Substance abuse treatment groups can be found in many general hospitals and local mental health clinics, and in employee assistance programs at work sites, should a teenager be in the paid workforce. Alcoholics Anonymous programs listed in the local white pages offer a variety of services for addicted young people (Young Peoples' AA), for nonaddicted adult family members (Alanon, Adult Children of Alcoholics), and for nonaddicted young family members (Alateen).

Narcotics Anonymous provides similar support groups for persons addicted to the other types of drugs.

Substance abuse treatment is a fundamental treatment component in those cases where it is needed for the warning signs to be fully addressed. The substance abusing youngster may deny its importance. That is part of the illness. Parents and care givers should never underestimate the importance of treating substance abuse to prevent violence and to restore the child to a more normal life.

PTSD may also be successfully treated (Flannery, 1994a). Often these treatments are not utilized because much PTSD goes undetected, and because victims are ashamed of what has befallen them.

Again, parents and care givers can be very helpful in this regard if they recognize the warning signs of PTSD, or if they learn of actual traumatic events in the youngster's life. Again, successful treatment is built on restoring reasonable mastery, caring attachments, and a renewed meaning in life in spite of the ugliness associated with the violence in the child's life. Parents and care givers become an important first caring attachment in the recovery process. There are also steps for restoring reasonable mastery that parents and care givers can include, such as helping the victim restore a more normal daily routine, or joining in needed relaxation exercises to reduce the physiological arousal associated with the aftermath of traumatic events. However, even here, some victims may feel frightened and vulnerable in a relaxed state. For these, aerobic exercise (after medical clearance) may be helpful, but for those with panic disorder aerobic exercises will increase the panic attacks and soft music may be a helpful substitute. (See Flannery [1994a] for a discussion of how to choose the best form of relaxation exercises in any given case.)

At some point, the youngster will need to address the violent episode directly. This is best left in the hands of professionally trained trauma counselors. This specialist will review the facts of what has happened with the child, help the child to grieve over the event, and then help the child to develop a new meaning in life so that normal functioning is restored. It is important that the therapist be trained in the use of psychological trauma interventions, as these skills differ from those utilized in general counseling interventions. Local professional medical and counseling societies can provide the names of such trauma specialists.

Conduct disorder is usually the most difficult issue to resolve because the extent of the child's anger and violence toward self or others is so intense. These are our most troubled children, and professional assistance will almost surely be needed. There are some medicines that may help with the conduct disordered youngster's depressive and impulsive feelings, and residential placement outside of the home for a time may also be needed to provide for the child a structure that contains cognitive and behavioral disorganization. In the structured setting, the creating of needed attachments and the teaching of necessary social skills can proceed more effectively than in the community where the child may be still exposed to an antisocial peer group, a life of street crime, and a lifestyle of substance abuse.

Professionals in all disciplines are there to assist parents, teachers, counselors, and case managers in developing the best approach for a conduct disordered child.

5. Fostering a Meaningful Purpose in Life

The last guideline turns our attention to the child's value system and the basic attitudes that guide the child's life. The data and theories on youth violence that we have examined make a compelling case for seeking some semblance of balance between the current cultural values of primacy of self, material acquisition, and instant gratification, and the more traditional prosocial values of honesty, trustworthiness, personal responsibility, and respect for the rights of others. The Declaration of Independence, the great religions of the world, and the research on resilient children all suggest the importance of a balance between reasonable ambition and concern for the welfare of others. The research demonstrates that, even in our own age, the traditional values are best for the child's growth and success as well as for the integrity of families and communities (Bloom, 1996; Masten and Coatsworth, 1998).

Parents, teachers, and counselors can promote these values in children by direct teaching, by modeling prosocial behaviors in their own interactions with the young, and by encouraging children to volunteer to be of service to others. Visiting the elderly in a nursing home, serving meals to the homeless in a shelter, being a Big Brother or Big Sister are all examples of how children can learn from their own experience the importance of concern for others.

When faulty or negative values have been learned from previous dysfunctional attachments or life circumstances and have led to the development of the warning signs, prosocial values may be introduced in the process of grieving these previous losses.

Grieving is the five-stage process outlined in chapter 3, and proceeds in the following steps: an acknowledgement of the fact of the loss, an expression of feelings commonly associated with loss (anger, sadness, depression, and grief), an acceptance of the fact that life is now different after the loss, and the development of a new meaningful purpose in life after the loss. It is during this latter step in the process that negative, unhelpful values can be challenged and rethought, and more prosocial values instilled.

Sometimes youngsters talk through their grief, but frequently artwork or playing with toys may also be helpful mediums of expression. For example, at one point in my practice, I was counseling an eight-year-old boy who had been physically and sexually abused by both parents. He was an angry young boy at home, at school, and in my clinic office. He would come in, run around the room, jump on the chairs, and try to eat the contents in my waste basket. He could not or would not talk about the abuse, so I chose toys as a way of helping him to express his anger in more focused ways and to begin to challenge his attitude that the world was a totally dangerous place.

We played cowboys and Indians with little toy representations. He chose to be the cowboys who were the good guys, and I was assigned to be the hostile Indians. After several episodes of losing, through the medium of the toys, I introduced one of the Indians as the medicine man, a doctor who helped the other Indians get better. I would patch up my wounded Indians who would live to fight another day. After a few more skirmishes, the youngster wanted a medicine man doctor for his cowboys. This was easily arranged, and now the child had at least one symbolic adult who could help him. In time, we were able to discuss the horror of his abuse and he was able to learn that not all adults were mean and destructive.

With these five guidelines incorporated as needed into the intervention program for a troubled young person, the parent, teacher, counselor, the case manager, and the entire adult care giving team have put in place the necessary structures and processes to resolve the warning signs. What is needed now is patience, time, and repeated learning trials until the child or teenager has mastered these steps, resolved the warning signs, and is ready to move on in life.

Preventing Youth Violence: Some Final Thoughts

This book began by noting that youth violence was a national public health epidemic, and certainly the statistics on youth violence are both chilling and depressing in confirming the types and extent of these acts. For some of us, the headlines of youth violence in schools and communities make us understand the seriousness of this matter. For others of us, there are personal experiences with violence among the young that impress upon us the extent of this epidemic.

In the two years that I was doing the basic research for this book, three of my colleagues had one of their children murdered by another young person. Three boys cut down in the springtime of their lives. Three other young males who will probably spend their lives in jail. Six families whose lives will be forever shattered. My colleagues were good hardworking people who spent long hours attentive to the task of child rearing. They reared good children with good values, and the future was promising for each child, for the parents, and for society as a whole. In three instants, each was gone forever. These deaths did not make national headlines, but they are part of our national epidemic. What is equally distressing is that my personal experience is not dissimilar from that of many other children and adults. The national epidemic is enveloping all of us. One by one. Event by event.

We have reviewed the extent of youth violence, its various causes, and the concept of the anomic cycle of violence as a way of having some general understanding of what is happening to our children in this era of intense, postindustrial, social change. We have considered the continuum of early, serious, and urgent warning signs, and how they are placed in order of increasing severity to illustrate how unattended early warning signs become worse over time. The warning signs are many and recognizable, and have often been there for several years. Finally, we reviewed the basic guidelines to remedy these issues and to restore our young people to more normal growth and development.

Rearing children, as we have seen, is difficult. It requires time, love, attention, work, and money. As a nation we must find a balance between pursuing material goods and allowing the needed hours for successful child rearing. Our children are our future. They should not be an endangered species. With the collective efforts of parents, teachers, and counselors, youth violence need not be the war that never ends.

APPENDIX A

National Associations for Preventing Youth Violence: Select Listing

Listed below is a representative sample of national associations and societies that are interested in preventing youth violence. They are listed by topics, and the reader should feel free to contact these groups for information or direction. This listing is by no means exhaustive of the possibilities available to citizens. Similar state and municipal organizations may be found in local telephone directories.

Counseling Societies

American Counseling
Association
5999 Stevenson Ave.
Alexandria, VA 22304

American Nurses Association
600 Maryland Avenue, SW
Suite 100 West
Washington, DC 20024

American Psychiatric
Association
1400 K Street, NW
Washington, DC 20005

American Psychological
Association
750 First Street, NE
Washington, DC 20002

American School Counselor
Association
801 N. Fairfax St.
Suite 310
Alexandria, VA 22314

National Association of Social
Workers
750 First Street, NE
Washington, DC 20002

Discrimination

American Civil Liberties Union
Foundation (ACLU)
1875 Connecticut Ave., NW
Washington, DC 20009

Antidefamation League Of
B'Nai B'rith
823 United Nations Plaza
New York, NY 10017

NAACP Legal Defense and
Educational Fund
1275 K Street, NW
No. 301
Washington, DC 20005

National Institute Against
Prejudice and Violence
31 South Greene Street
Baltimore, MD 21201

Domestic Violence

Center for Prevention of Sexual
and Domestic Violence
936 N. 34th Street
Suite 200
Seattle, WA 98103

Children's Defense Fund
25 E Street, NW
Washington, DC 20001

Family Violence Prevention
Fund
383 Rhode Island Street
San Francisco, CA 94103

National Center on Child
Abuse and Neglect
U.S. Department of Health and
Human Services
P.O. Box 1182
Washington, DC 20013

National Clearinghouse on
Child Abuse and Family
Violence
1155 Connecticut Avenue, NW
Suite 400
Washington, DC 20036

National Coalition Against
Domestic Violence
P.O. Box 34103
Washington, DC 20043

National Committee to Prevent
Child Abuse
332 S. Michigan Avenue
Suite 1600
Chicago, IL 60604

National Organization for
Victim Assistance
1757 Park Road, NW
Washington, DC 20010

Education

American Federation of
Teachers
555 New Jersey Avenue, NW
Washington, DC 20001

American School Health
Association
7263 State Route 43
P.O. Box 708
Kent, OH 44240

National Alliance for Safe
Schools
9344 Lanham Severn Rd.
No. 104
Lanham, MD 20706

National Association for
Education of Young Children
1509 16th Street, NW
Washington, DC 20036

National Education Association
1201 16th Street, NW
Washington, DC 20036

School and Community Safety
Society of America
1900 Association Drive
Reston, VA 20191

Grief and Loss

American Association of
Suicidology
4201 Connecticut Avenue, NW
Suite 310
Washington, DC 20008

Bereaved Parents USA
P.O. Box 95
Park Forest, IL 60466

National Directory of
Bereavement
Support Groups and Services
P.O. Box 75115
Forest Hills, N.Y.

National Hospice Organization
1901 North Moore Street
Suite 901
Alexandria, VA 22209

National Sudden Infant Death
Syndrome Alliance
1314 Bedford Avenue
Suite 210
Baltimore, MD 21208

Parents of Murdered Children,
Inc.
100 E. 8th Street
Cincinnati, OH 45202

Legal

Center on Battered Women's
Legal Services
105 Chambers Street
New York, NY 10007

National Association of
Counsel for Children
1205 O'Neida Street
Denver, CO 80220

Federal Bureau of Investigation
10th Street and Pennsylvania
Ave., NW
Washington, DC 20535

National Bar Association
1225 11th Street, NW
Washington, DC 20001

Media

Center for Media and Public
Affairs
2101 L Street, NW
Washington, DC 20037

Morality in Media
475 Riverside Drive
Suite 405
New York, NY 10115

Free Press Association
P.O. Box 15548
Columbus, OH 43215

National Council for Families
and Television
3801 Barkam Boulevard
Suite 300
Los Angeles, CA 90068

Substance Abuse

Alcoholics Anonymous (AA)
P.O. Box 459
Grand Central Station
New York, NY 10163

Narcotics Anonymous
World Service Office, Inc.
P.O. Box 999
Van Nuys, CA 91409

Al-Anon Family Group
Headquarters
1372 Broadway
New York, NY 10018

National Federation of Parents
for Drug-Free Youth
8730 Georgia Avenue
Suite 200
Silver Spring, MD 20910

National Institute on Alcohol
Abuse and Alcoholism (NIAAA)
Room 16-105
Parklawn Building
5600 Fisher Lane
Rockville, MD 20857

National Institute on Drug
Abuse (NIDA)
Room 10-05
Parklawn Building
5600 Fisher Lane
Rockville, MD 20857

Youth Violence

Center for Study of Youth
Policy
University of Michigan
School of Social Work
1015 Huron Street
Ann Arbor, MI 48104

Community Youth Gang
Services
144 S. Fitterly Avenue
Los Angeles, CA 90022

Family Resource Coalition
200 S. Michigan Avenue
Suite 1520
Chicago, IL 60604

MAD DAD
2221 N. 24th Street
Omaha, NE 68110

Mothers Against Gangs
110 W. Madison Street
Chicago, IL 60602

National Clearinghouse On
Satanic Crime in America
USCCCN International, Inc.
P.O. Box 1185-Nixon Station
Edison, NJ 08818

National Council of Churches
Committee for Justice for
Children and Their Families
475 Riverside Drive
Room 848
New York, NY 10015

National Council of Juvenile
and Family Court Judges
P.O. Box 8970
University of Nevada
Reno, NV 89557

National Crime Prevention
Council
1700 K Street, NW
Washington, DC 20006

National School Safety Center
4165 Thousand Oaks Blvd.
Suite 290
Westlake Village, CA 91362

U.S. Department of Justice
Juvenile Justice and
Delinquency Prevention
633 Indiana Avenue, NW
Washington, DC 20531

U.S. Drug Enforcement
Administration
1405 I Street, NW
Washington, DC 20537

Victims of Violence

American Humane Association
Children's Division
63 Iverness Drive E.
Englewood, CO 80112

International Society for
Traumatic Stress Studies
60 Revere Drive
Suite 500
Northbrook, IL 60062

C. H. Kempe National Center for
Prevention and Treatment
of Child Abuse
1205 Oneida Avenue
Denver, CO 80220

National Victim Center
309 West 7th Street
Suite 705
Fort Worth, TX 76102

Select Readings

Chapter 1: Children: Our Endangered Species

Berry, W. *Another Turn of the Crank*. Washington, D.C.: Counterpoint, 1995.

Coccaro, E. F. "Impulsive Aggression: A Behavior in Search of Clinical Definiton." *Harvard Review of Psychiatry*, 5 (1998): 336-39.

Dobrin, A., Wiersema, B., Loftin, C., and McDowall, D. *Statistical Handbook of Violence in America*. Phoenix, AZ: Ornyx Press, 1996.

Flannery, R. B., Jr. *Post-Traumatic Stress Disorder: The Victim's Guide to Healing and Recovery*. New York: Crossroad, 1994a.

———. *Violence in the Workplace*. New York: Crossroad, 1995

Hewlitt, S. A. *When the Bough Breaks: The Cost of Neglecting Our Children*. New York: Basic Books, 1991.

Kunz, J., and Bahr, S. J. "A Profile of Parental Homicide Against Children." *Journal of Family Violence*, 11 (1996): 347-62.

Straus, M. A., and Gelles, R. J. *Physical Violence in American Families: Risk Factors and Adaptations to Violence in 8,145 Families*. Edited with Assistance of Christine Smith. New Brunswick, N.J.: Transaction Publishers, 1992.

Widom, C. S. "The Cycle of Violence." *Science*, 244 (1989): 160-66.

Wolfgang, M., Figlio, R. M., and Sellin, T. *Delinquency in a Birth Cohort*. Chicago: University of Chicago Press, 1972.

Chapter 2: Armed and Dangerous: Theories of Youth Violence

Archer, J. (Ed.). *Male Violence*. New York: Routledge, 1994.

Bouchard, T. J., Jr. "Genes, Environment, and Personality." *Science*, 264 (1994): 1700-1701.

Derber, C. *The Wilding of America: How Greed and Violence Are Eroding Our Nation and Character*. New York: St. Martin's Press, 1996.

Drucker, P. "The Age of Social Transformation." *Atlantic Monthly*, 276 (1994): 53-80.

Durkheim, É. *Suicide: A Study in Sociology*. Trans: J. Spaulding and G. Simpson. New York: The Free Press, 1951.

Flannery, R. B., Jr. *Violence in America: Coping with Drugs, Distressed Families, Inadequate Schooling, and Acts of Hate.* New York: Continuum, 1997.

Goldstein, A. *Addiction: From Biology to Drug Policy.* New York: Freeman, 1994.

Prothrow-Stith, D. *Deadly Consequences.* New York: Harper Collins, 1991.

Thurow, L. *The Future of Capitalism: How Today's Economic Forces Shape Tomorrow's World.* New York: Morrow, 1996.

Wekesser, C. *Violence in the Media: Current Controversies.* San Diego: Greenhaven, 1995.

Chapter 3: Early Warning Signs: Disruptions in Mastery, Attachments, and Meaning

Antonovsky, A. *Health, Stress, and Coping.* San Francisco: Jossey-Bass, 1979.

Becker, E. *The Denial of Death.* New York: The Free Press, 1973.

Bowlby, J. *Attachment and Loss, Vol. I: Attachment.* New York: Basic Books, 1973.

Flannery, R. B., Jr. *Becoming Stress-Resistant through the Project SMART Program.* New York: Crossroad, 1994b.

Kübler-Ross, E. *On Death and Dying.* New York: Macmillan, 1969.

Lynch, J.J. The Broken Heart: *The Medical Consequences of Loneliness.* New York: Basic Books, 1977.

Masten, A. S., and Coatsworth, J. D. "The Development of Competence in Favorable and Unfavorable Environments." *American Psychologist,* 53 (1998), 205-20.

Sagan, L. N. *The Health of Nations: True Causes of Sickness and Well-Being.* New York: Basic Books, 1987.

Scarr, S. "American Child Care Today." *American Psychologist,* 53 (1998): 95-108.

Wallerstein, J., and Blakeslee, S. *Second Chances: Men, Women, and Children a Decade after Divorce.* New York: Tichnor and Fields, 1989.

Chapter 4: Serious Warning Signs: Depression, Substance Abuse, Posttraumatic Stress Disorder

Cicchetti, D., and Toth, S. L. "The Development of Depression in Children and Adolescents." *American Psychologist,* 53 (1998): 221-241.

Collins, J. J., and Bailey, S. L. "Traumatic Stress Disorder and Violent Behavior." *Journal of Traumatic Stress*, 3 (1990): 203-220.

Everly, G. S., Jr., and Laiting, J. M. *Psychotraumatology: Key Papers and Core Concepts in Post-Traumatic Stress*. New York: Plenum, 1995.

Justice, B. *Who Gets Sick: How Beliefs, Moods, and Thoughts Affect Your Health*. Los Angeles: J. P. Tarcher, 1988.

Khantzian, E.J. "The Self-Medication Hypothesis of Substance Use Disorders: A Reconsideration of Recent Applications." *Harvard Review of Psychiatry*, 4 (1997): 231-44.

Rothman, J. C. *The Bereaved Parent's Survival Guide*. New York: Continuum, 1997.

van der Kolk, B. A. (Ed.) *Psychological Trauma*. Washington, D.C.: American Psychiatric Press, 1987.

Wilson, J. P. *Trauma, Transformation, and Healing: An Integrative Approach to Theory, Research, and Post-Traumatic Therapy*. New York: Brunner/Mazel, 1989.

Woodarski, J. S. *Preventive Health Services for Adolescents*. Springfield, IL: Charles Thomas, 1989.

Zigler, E. F., Kagan, S. L., and Hall, N. W. *Children, Families, and Government: Preparing for the Twenty-First Century*. New York: Cambridge University Press, 1997.

Chapter 5: Urgent Warning Signs: Conduct Disorder

American Psychiatric Association. *Diagnostic and Statistical Manual of Mental Disorders*. Fourth Edition. Washington, D.C.: American Psychiatric Association, 1994.

Cleckly, H. *The Mask of Sanity: An Attempt to Clarify Some Issues about the So-Called Psychopathic Personality*. St. Louis, MO: Mosely, 1955.

DeBecker, G. *The Gift of Fear: Survival Strategies that Protect us from Violence*. Boston: Little, Brown, 1997.

Farrington, D. P. "Childhood, Adolescent, and Adult Features of Violent Males." In Huseman, L. R. (Ed.), *Aggressive Behavior: Current Perspectives*. New York: Plenum Press, 1994, 215-40.

Kay, P., Estepa, A., and Desetta, A. (Eds.) *Things Get Hectic: Teens Write about the Violence That Surrounds Them*. New York: Touchstone, 1998.

Magid, K., and McKelvey, C. A. *High Risk Children Without a Conscience*. New York: Bantam, 1987.

Margolis, J. A. *Teen Crime Wave: A Growing Problem.* Springfield, NJ: Enslow Publishers, 1997.

Samenow, S. E. *Before It's Too Late: Why Some Kids Get into Trouble— and What Parents Can Do about It.* New York: Times Books, 1989.

Sorokin, P. A. *The Crisis of Our Age.* New York: Dutton, 1941.

Stewart, G. B. *The Other America: Teens in Prison.* San Diego: Lucent Books, 1997.

Chapter 6: Preventing Youth Violence

Bloom, N. "Primary Prevention and Resiliency: Changing Paradigms and Changing Lives." In Hampton, R. L., Jenkins, P., and Gullotta, T. P. *Preventing Violence in America. Issues in Children's and Families Lives.* Vol. 4. Thousand Oaks, CA: Sage, 1996. Pg. 87-114.

Crespi, T. D. "Violent Children and Adolescents: Facing the Treatment Crisis in Child and Family Interaction." *Family Therapy,* 23 (1996): 43-50.

Hochschild, A., with Machung, A. *The Second Shift: Working Parents and the Revolution at Home.* New York: Viking, 1989.

Laidler, K. A. Joe, and Hunt, G. "Violence and Social Organization in Female Gangs." *Social Justice,* 24 (1997): 148-69.

Morrison, B. *As If: A Crime, A Trial, A Question of Childhood.* New York: Picador USA, 1997.

Pajer, K. A. "What Happens to 'Bad' Girls? A Review of the Adult Outcomes of Antisocial Adolescent Girls," *American Journal of Psychiatry,* 155 (1998): 862-70.

Stacey, W., and Shupe, A. *The Family Secret: Domestic Violence in America.* Boston: Beacon Press, 1983.

Weinstein, S. *Family Beyond Family: The Surrogate Parent in Schools and Other Community Agencies.* New York: Haworth Press, 1995.

Wilson, K. J. *When Violence Begins at Home: A Comprehensive Guide to Understanding and Enduring Domestic Violence.* Alameda, CA: Hunter House, 1997.

Yurgelun-Todd, D. "Brain and Psyche: The Neurobiology of Self." Paper presented at the Whitehead Institute Press Seminar, Boston, 1998.

Index

About the Author

Raymond B. Flannery, Jr., Ph.D., F.A.P.M., a licensed clinical psychologist, is Associate Clinical Professor of Psychology, Department of Psychiatry, Harvard Medical School in Boston, and Adjunct Assistant Professor of Psychiatry, University of Massachusetts Medical School, Worcester. For over thirty years he has been a counselor and professional educator of business persons, professionals, health care providers, and the general public about life stress, psychological trauma, and violence in the community and in the workplace. He has lectured nationally and is the author of over seventy papers in the medical and science journals.

Dr. Flannery is also the author of five previous books for interested professionals and the general public. *Becoming Stress-Resistant through the Project SMART Program* (New York: Continuum, 1990, and Crossroad, 1994) is for those wanting to learn how to cope effectively with the general stress of life in today's age. It is based on a twelve-year study of 1,200 persons and how the most adaptive among them coped with life stress. His second book, *Post-Traumatic Stress Disorder: The Victim's Guide to Healing and Recovery* (New York: Crossroad, 1992, 1994), is the first book written for victims of psychological trauma, and outlines effective coping strategies for persons seeking to recover from the severe stress of traumatic events. *Violence in the Workplace* (New York: Crossroad, 1995) is his third book and the first to examine the general nature and causes of work site violence and the first to present a threefold approach to reduce the risk of its occurrence, and to contain its aftermath, when it does occur. His fourth book, *Violence in America: Coping with Drugs, Distressed Families, Inadequate Schooling, and Acts of Hate* (New York: Continuum, 1997) is the first comprehensive review of the theories of the causes of violence, and the first to present a basic overview of what business, government, families, schools, and religion can do to stop its spread. His fifth work, *The Assaulted Staff Action Program (ASAP): Coping with the Psychological Aftermath of Violence* (Ellicott City, MD: Chevron Publishing Corporation, 1998) outlines a crisis intervention debriefing program that Dr. Flannery designed for victims of violence.

Dr. Flannery and his wife live in the suburbs of Boston.

The Continuum of Warning Signs

Early Warning Signs	Biological Markers
	Disrupted Attachments: Disruptions in Family Unit, Dysfunctional Family Unit, Absence of Peer Group, Disrupted Relationships at School or in the Neighborhood
	Disruptions in Reasonable Mastery: Deficiencies in Personal Growth, Interpersonal Growth, Academics
	Disruptions in Meaning: Disavows Prosocial Values, Disregard for Others
Serious Warning Signs	Depression (with Suicidal Thinking)
	Substance Abuse
	Posttraumatic Stress Disorder
Urgent Warning Signs	Conduct Disorder

Carol J. Adams and Marie M. Fortune, editors
VIOLENCE AGAINST WOMEN AND CHILDREN
A Christian Theological Sourcebook

"If you read only one book this year, let it be this one. . . ."
—*National Catholic Reporter*

Raymond B. Flannery, Jr., Ph.D.
VIOLENCE IN AMERICA
Coping with Drugs, Distressed Families, Inadequate Schooling, and Acts of Hate

"In this academic but accessible overview of violence, clinical psychologist Flannery (*Post-Traumatic Stress Disorder: The Victim's Guide to Healing and Recovery*) presents an impressive array of sociological studies and crime statistics to support his contention that violence in the U.S. has become a major public-health problem 'of epidemic proportion.' He argues convincingly that to slow the rate of violence, our major institutions must contribute to a solution."—*Publishers Weekly*

Sigmund Freud
PSYCHOLOGICAL WRITINGS AND LETTERS

Edited by Sander L. Gilman, this volume includes: "Infant Sexuality," "Psychopathology of Everyday Life." "The Uncanny," "A Difficulty in the Path of Psychoanalysis," and other important works.

William E. Prendergast, Ph.D.
SEXUAL ABUSE OF CHILDREN AND ADOLESCENTS
A Preventive Guide for Parents, Teachers, and Counselors

"Dr. Prendergast's helping method is pragmatic rather than being based on a particular model. It is somewhat reminiscent of Glasser's Reality Therapy in its directness and wise use of confrontation"
—Alan Keith-Lucas, Ph.D.

Juliet Cassuto Rothman
THE BEREAVED PARENTS' SURVIVAL GUIDE

"This book is beautifully written. The insights shared here will bring comfort, strength, and hope to bereaved parents everywhere, in each of their many stages of grief. Juliet gives you the ability to believe that you will once again enjoy being part of mainstream life. Thank you, Juliet."

—Janet Tyler, bereaved parent and chapter leader of Bereaved Parents, U.S.A.

At your bookstore or order from
The Continuum Publishing Company
370 Lexington Avenue
New York, NY 10017

www.continuum-books.com